The Prime Ministers of Canada

Grades 4-8

Written by Frances Stanford
Illustrated by Ric Ward and S&S Learning Materials

ISBN 1-55035-721-2
Copyright 2002
Revised April 2006
All Rights Reserved * Printed in Canada

Permission to Reproduce

Permission is granted to the individual teacher who purchases one copy of this book to reproduce the student activity material for use in his/her classroom only. Reproduction of these materials for an entire school or for a school system, or for other colleagues or for commercial sale is <u>strictly prohibited</u>. No part of this publication may be transmitted in any form or by any means, electronic, mechanical, recording or otherwise without the prior written permission of the publisher. "We acknowledge the financial support of the Government of Canada through the Book Publishing Industry Development Program (BPIDP) for this project."

Published in Canada by:
S&S Learning Materials
15 Dairy Avenue
Napanee, Ontario
K7R 1M4
www.sslearning.com

At a Glance

Learning Expectations	Points to Ponder	Explore History	What Have You Learned?	Quizzes 1 & 2
Language Skills				
• Reading comprehension	•	•	•	•
• Summarizing events/details	•	•	•	
• Recalling information	•		•	•
• Expressing personal views	•	•		
Reasoning & Critical Thinking Skills				
• Making comparisons	•	•	•	
• Developing opinions and personal interpretations	•	•		
• Making inferences (e.g., why events occurred)	•	•		
• Developing research skills		•		
• Analyzing and evaluating historical information	•	•		
• Recognizing the validity of differing points of view	•	•		
• Identifying causes of conflict	•	•		
Understanding				
• Name the prime ministers of Canada and their role in Canadian history	•	•	•	•
• Understand what is involved in being a prominent politician	•	•		
• Develop an appreciation for the political system of Canada	•	•	•	
• Understand the connection between government, policies, and the laws that affect one's life	•	•		
• Have knowledge of some of the events that have shaped Canada including Confederation, and two World Wars	•	•		•
• Be able to discuss what each prime minister did during office	•	•		•
• Appreciate some of the benefits of different actions taken by various prime ministers	•	•		•
• Understand some of the character traits that successful prime ministers have possessed	•	•		
• Develop increased understanding in the issue of the separatist movement	•	•		
• Understand some of the complexities in international relations between Canada, Britain, USA, and other countries	•	•		

 # The Prime Ministers of Canada

Table of Contents

Learning Outcomes 4
Teaching Suggestions 4
Glossary 5
Introduction 6
Sir John A. Macdonald 10
Alexander Mackenzie 13
Sir John Joseph Caldwell Abbott 16
Sir John Sparrow David Thompson 19
Mackenzie Bowell 22
Sir Charles Tupper 24
Sir Wilfrid Laurier 26
Sir Robert Laird Borden 30
Arthur Meighen 33
William Lyon Mackenzie King 36
Richard Bedford Bennett 40
Louis St. Laurent 43
John George Diefenbaker 46
Lester Bowles Pearson 49
Pierre Elliott Trudeau 52
Charles Joseph Clark/John Turner 55
Martin Brian Mulroney/Avril Kim Campbell 58
Jean Chrétien 61
Paul Martin 64
Stephen Harper 67
What Have You Learned? 69
Quiz 1 70
Quiz 2 72
Answer Key 73
Sketches of the Prime Ministers 78

The Prime Ministers of Canada

Learning Outcomes

At the end of this resource, students will:
- be able to name the prime ministers of Canada
- understand what is involved in holding such a prominent office
- be able to tell what each prime minister did during his/her term of office
- demonstrate the ability to discuss events which took place in Canada and the world under each administration
- be able to express judgments regarding the benefits of different actions taken by various prime ministers

Teaching Suggestions

- Teachers should have a large map of Canada on a wall in the classroom to pinpoint the location of various events which took place during each prime minister's term in office.
- This resource may be used when studying the Canadian government, elections or Confederation.
- An ideal time for using this resource would be during an election campaign.
- It would be beneficial for students if the teacher could make arrangements for a visit to the class by the Member of Parliament for the electoral district in which the school is located.
- The students should also be able to view one of the proceedings from the House of Commons on the appropriate TV channel.
- If it is possible, a tour of the Parliament buildings and the House of Commons would give the students a better idea of how the government of Canada works. Another possibility would be to use slides or pictures of Ottawa in class.
- A variety of material on Canada, Ottawa, and the prime ministers should be made available to the students.
- Have a chart on the bulletin board with the names of the prime ministers where students can add information about each prime minister as he/she is studied.
- Students' writings and drawings should be displayed in the classroom.
- As a culminating activity for this resource, students can pretend to be a prime minister of his/her choice and deliver a speech during his/her term of office. A website which can be used for speeches is www.collectionscanada.ca/primeministers.
- There are also quizzes on each of the prime ministers at this site that the students can do.

The Prime Ministers of Canada

Glossary of Selected Terms

Auditor General: this is the person, with his/her staff, responsible for making sure that the government is held to account for its use of public funds and doesn't waste the people's money.

backbencher: MPs who do not have as much power to influence government policy, do not have a special appointment or office, and are not front spokespersons for their party.

by-election: a special election that is held to fill a seat that has become vacant in between general elections.

"called to the bar": a certificate issued by a provincial Law Society that officially makes someone who has studied law and passed their exams a solicitor who is able to practice law in the courts.

Canadian Constitution: is the chief document outlining Canada's basic laws and how it operates. It includes how the government is run, and the civil rights (personal rights) of Canadian people.

capitalism: an economic system whereby there is little government control over the prices of goods. Instead, prices fluctuate by how much people will pay for goods, and how much people are willing to sell them for.

concription: when governments force their citizens, usually males, to enlist in the military.

constituency: a group of voters from a certain area, known as a **riding**, that elect a member of Parliament to represent them.

depression: a time when the economics of a country is not in good shape; when there is not much money coming into the system. In the 1930s the Great Depression resulted in many people being without work, and there was great shortage of food and goods.

free trade: is a policy that allows things to be bought and sold internationally without **tariffs** (taxes on imports)

House of Commons: is that part of Canada's Parliament (government) that consists of all the elected members of Parliament. The House of Commons holds the most power over Canada's laws and policies. They meet in the Houses of Parliament in Ottawa.

Legislation: laws that have been enacted, or are being considered for enactment, in government. When a law is suggested it is called a **bill**, until it is accepted or rejected by Parliament.

Privy Council: a group of advisors to the Queen

secret ballot: a method of voting that keeps the vote hidden and private so that no-one else knows who the voter chooses. This is one way to help keep an election fair.

Senate: a group of politicians that are appointed as part of Parliament. They do not have a lot of power, and though their approval is required to pass a bill, they rarely go against the House of Commons.

separatist movement: a group of people that wish to have Quebec become its own country instead of being a province of Canada

social welfare: government provided assistance to individual citizens, including health care, education, financial support, etc.

Solicitor General: a position in provincial government that is responsible for prisons and police. There is no longer a Solicitor General in federal government in Canada.

spoils system: occurs when a newly elected leader appoints people to government positions because they worked hard to help them get elected, rather than because they would be good for the job.

union: an organization of a group of workers in an industry that fights to get and keep better working conditions and wages.

 # The Prime Ministers of Canada

Introduction: The Making of a Prime Minister

This is a book about the prime ministers of Canada. Canada is a democracy and a constitutional monarchy, which means that the head of state in Canada is HRH Queen Elizabeth II, the ruler of Great Britain, who is also the Queen of Britain, Australia, New Zealand and many other countries. Every act passed by the Government of Canada is done so in the name of the Queen or the Crown. The representative of the Queen in Canada is the Governor-General.

The leader of the Government in Canada is called the prime minister. This term means "first among equals": even though all members of the Cabinet are equal, the prime minister is more powerful than the others. The prime minister is normally a member of the House of Commons. A non-member can hold the office but must win a seat in the House of Commons through an election. The prime minister can lose his/her seat in an election, but must win another seat very promptly. The traditional way of doing this has been to arrange to have a member of the majority party resign to allow the prime minister to run in a special election, called a by-election, in that district.

The prime minister is appointed by the Governor-General. Ordinarily this appointment is automatic. The leader of the party that wins the most seats in a general election becomes the prime minister of Canada. The prime minister then gives some of the members who have been elected by the people special jobs or portfolios. These members are called ministers and are placed in charge of the main government departments which are also called ministries. Some examples of ministries are Fisheries, Finance, Immigration, and Labour. These ministers and the prime minister form what is called the Cabinet.

What Does a Prime Minister Do?

The prime minister and the Cabinet work together to decide the laws of Canada and what new programs should be implemented. The duties of the prime minister are not specified in the Constitution. Generally, he/she follows the traditions of Parliament performing the duties that a prime minister has always done.

• Government Leader

The prime minister first and foremost must lead the government of Canada. He/She must speak in Parliament, to news reporters, and at national and international meetings. He/She decides what bills Cabinet ministers bring before the House of Commons, appoints senators to the Senate, recommends the Governor-General to the Queen, chooses lieutenant-governors for the provinces, and judges to the Supreme and federal courts.

The Prime Ministers of Canada

• Cabinet Leader

The prime minister has to also make sure that the Cabinet ministers he/she appoints do their job by holding regular meetings. It is in these meetings that the prime minister approves the bills that are to be voted on in the House of Commons.

• Member of Parliament

In addition to running the government and ensuring that all the ministries are running smoothly, the prime minister is also an elected member of the House of Commons. This means that he/she is also responsible for a particular electoral riding in a province of Canada. He/She has to make sure that the interests and concerns of the citizens of that riding are looked after.

• Party Leader

In order to be the leader of the Canadian government, a person must first win the leadership of political party. However, the prime minister must serve the interests of the country as a whole, not just a particular region, even if it means disagreeing with some of his/her Cabinet ministers. As party leader, the prime minister hosts and attends many party meetings and fund-raising events, and works to keep the party well-organized between elections.

• International Leader

The prime minister of Canada is also a world leader serving on many international committees and is required to do a lot of travelling outside Canada to attend meetings and help make decisions which affect the entire world.

 # The Prime Ministers of Canada

Becoming a Prime Minister

A person in Canada cannot automatically decide to become the prime minister of the country. A person in any part of the country can decide to enter politics at the time of a general election or a by-election. He/She must win the nomination to run for the party of his/her choice and be elected to represent that particular electoral riding by a majority of votes from the people. Once elected, the person then becomes a member of Parliament in the House of Commons in Ottawa.

Depending on the qualifications the representative might have, he/she could be asked by the prime minister to sit in the Cabinet in charge of a portfolio. When a leadership review is called, the person can then decide to run for the position of leader of the party. This requires lobbying other members of Parliament and a lot of travelling throughout Canada to win the votes and support of the general populace. If he/she is chosen to lead the party and that party holds the majority of seats in the House of Commons, then the Governor-General will appoint him/her to the position of prime minister.

The prime minister of Canada must call an election every five years. Elections can also be called at any time within that period. If the party of which the prime minister is the leader wins the most seats, then he/she will retain the position. There is no limit on the number of terms a person can serve as prime minister and a defeated prime minister can return to power in another election.

Being a prime minister means a loss of privacy. Everything a prime minister does and says becomes public knowledge and is often criticized very harshly in the press. The job is also dangerous, as many times the prime minister has to make decisions that are not popular with the people. Therefore, the prime minister is heavily guarded whenever he/she is out in public.

Since Canada became a country in 1867, there have been 22 different prime ministers. Several of these have served more than once and several have served for only a short period of time. There have been popular and unpopular prime ministers and some unpopular decisions have been made since the first prime minister took office in 1867.

 # The Prime Ministers of Canada

Name _____ **Date** _____

Points to Ponder

1. What does the term "prime minister" mean? _____
   _____
   _____
   _____

2. How is the prime minister of Canada chosen? _____
   _____
   _____
   _____
   _____
   _____

3. What are the duties of the prime minister of Canada?
   _____
   _____
   _____
   _____

4. Based on what you have read about the position of prime minister, would you like to be the prime minister of Canada? Why or why not?
   _____
   _____
   _____
   _____
   _____

© S&S Learning Materials   SSJ1-47 The Prime Ministers of Canada

The Prime Ministers of Canada

Sir John A. Macdonald (1815 - 1891)
Prime Minister: 1867 - 1873, 1878 - 1891

John Alexander Macdonald was born January 10, 1815, in Glasgow, Scotland. He moved to Kingston, Upper Canada with his parents when he was five years old. His father, Hugh Macdonald, had failed at business ventures in Scotland and he was not very successful in Upper Canada. It was largely through the efforts of his mother, Helen, that John received a good education. At the age of ten, he was sent to the Midland Grammar School in Kingston and later to a small school operated by a Scottish clergyman. When he was fifteen, he articled to become a lawyer with George MacKenzie.

In 1835, at the age of twenty, he opened his own law office. He soon earned a reputation for flair and ingenuity in his legal work and entered corporate law in 1840, becoming the solicitor for companies such as the Commercial Bank of the Midland District and the Trust and Loan Company of Upper Canada. By 1842, his law office had become one of the busiest in Canada.

Macdonald had a lively mind and an enormous range of knowledge. He read widely and added to his speeches funny references from his reading. When he was depressed or when his affairs were in disarray, he sometimes got drunk, although he was not a chronic drinker. Sometimes he drank in a spirit of companionship with his friends.

Macdonald entered politics in 1844, when he was elected to the Legislative Assembly of Upper Canada as the Conservative member for Kingston. In those early years, he opposed a Canadian government that was responsible to itself, rather than the monarchy, and he disagreed with allowing more people to vote. He felt that these would weaken the authority of the government. He opposed the power of the Family Compact, a group of royalists who dominated the power in the Government of Upper Canada. He helped to build a more moderate group, the Liberal-Conservatives, and became Receiver General in the government in 1847. However, the government was defeated over the King's College Endowment Bill. Macdonald was one of the few Conservatives who were returned to the Legislative Assembly after the Reformers won the majority of seats.

From the opposition side of the government, Macdonald worked to increase his influence among the Conservatives and to broaden the boundaries of the party to allow more people to become members. He was willing to work with the French Canadian politicians of Lower Canada, especially his rival, Georges-Étienne Cartier. This alliance allowed him to rally French Canadian support for the coalition government of the mid-1860s. The Great Coalition Government of 1864

The Prime Ministers of Canada

was supported by three of the four political parties of the united Province of Canada: the Bleus of Canada East and the Conservatives and Reformers of Canada West. Their aim was to form a confederation of the British North American colonies.

Macdonald did not initially support the idea of Confederation, but once he did, he pushed it forward. He took the lead at the Charlottetown, Quebec, and London conferences and was responsible for writing the Canadian Constitution.

Macdonald as Prime Minister

When Confederation was formed in 1867, John A. Macdonald became the first Prime Minister of Canada. He was also awarded a knighthood by Queen Victoria and was now Sir John A. Macdonald. During his first term of office from 1867-1873, he continued the work of building the new nation. In 1868-1869, he arranged better terms of union for Nova Scotia, bought the Hudson Bay Company's land, and added Manitoba and the Northwest Territories to Canada in 1869-1870, added British Columbia in 1871, created the Northwest Mounted Police in 1873, and brought Prince Edward Island into Confederation in 1873.

Macdonald fell from power in 1873 as a result of the Pacific Scandal. This centered around large amounts of money that the leading Conservatives had accepted as campaign funds from the railway promoters, who were competing for the rights to build the Canadian Pacific Railway. Macdonald claimed that he had not used any of the money personally, but his government was forced to resign in November of 1873. He tried to resign as leader of the party, but his supporters would not allow him to do so.

Macdonald was returned to power in the elections of 1878 and remained there for three terms until 1891. His major achievements during this time were the National Policy and the completion of the Canadian Pacific Railway. The National Policy was a program introduced in 1879 which was designed to promote Canadian industry by taxing imported goods.

Macdonald remained in politics despite his age. He won his last election in 1891 at the age of 76. He had introduced younger people into the government as the older members retired. One of his proudest moments was when he escorted his son, Hugh John Macdonald into the House as a new member of Parliament on April 29, 1891. The elder died of a stroke on June 6, 1891, still prime minister of Canada. Sir John A. Macdonald is known as the father of Confederation and is recognized as the father and founder of Canada.

The Prime Ministers of Canada   Sir John A. MacDonald

Name _____   **Date** _____

Points to Ponder

1. What qualities did John A. Macdonald possess that enabled him to succeed in his law practice?
   _____
   _____
   _____

2. What ideas was he opposed to when he first entered politics? Why?
   _____
   _____
   _____

3. Why did Macdonald decide to join forces with French Canadian politicians? _____
   _____
   _____

4. Make a list of the accomplishments of Sir John A. Macdonald during his terms as prime minister.
   _____
   _____
   _____
   _____
   _____

   Explore History

1. What were the first uniforms of the Royal Canadian Mounted Police?
2. What was the Pacific Scandal?
3. What was the importance of the National Policy?
4. Why was John A. Macdonald given a knighthood by Queen Victoria?

The Prime Ministers of Canada

Alexander Mackenzie (1822 - 1892)
Prime Minister: 1873 - 1878

Alexander Mackenzie was born on January 28, 1822, in Logierait, near Dunkeld, Scotland. His father died while Alexander was very young, so he had to go to work at the age of fourteen to support his mother and his brothers. He apprenticed to a stonemason and was fully trained by the time he was nineteen. He emigrated to Canada in 1842, partly because of shortage of work in Scotland and partly because his childhood sweetheart, Helen Neil, was emigrating to Canada, with her family. He settled in Sarnia, Upper Canada where he and his brother became builders. He married Helen in 1845 and after her death seven years later, he married Jane Sym in 1853.

As a stonemason and builder in Canada, he built a bomb-proof stone arch at Fort Henry in Kingston and worked on the Beauharnois Canal near Montreal. Many of his constructions still stand today. Some examples of these structures are the Welland Canal, the Martello Towers at Fort Henry, a church and a bank in Sarnia, and the courthouses and jails in Chatham and Sandwich. He also edited the Reformer paper, the *Lambton Shield*.

When an election was called in 1861, he decided to enter politics. The voters were familiar with him as a businessman and saw him as a sensible, hardworking, honest candidate. As a result he was elected to the Legislative Assembly for the Province of Canada. He was also elected to Canada's first Parliament in 1867 as a Liberal member. By 1873, he was the leader of the Liberal Party in the Government of Canada. A general election was called after the fall of the Macdonald government because of the Pacific Scandal. Mackenzie's Liberals gained the majority of seats in the House of Commons and he became the second prime minister of Canada.

MacKenzie as Prime Minister

On November 7, 1873, the Governor-General called on Mackenzie to form a government. MacKenzie became Prime Minister and also took on the Ministry of Public Works in order to supervise the railways. He oversaw the completion of the Intercolonial Railway between Atlantic Canada and Upper and Lower Canada, and the Parliament buildings, and established the Supreme Court of Canada in 1875. However, he did not approve of the Canadian Pacific Railway. As a result of his stalling on this matter, British Columbia threatened to withdraw from Confederation. To appease the situation, British Columbia accepted an annual subsidy until the railway was completed.

The Prime Ministers of Canada

MacKenzie was a very efficient administrator. He quickly introduced the secret ballot, straightened out the railway situation and sent George Brown to the United States to negotiate tariff concessions with that country. In 1874, he founded the Royal Military College and in 1878, he created the Office of the Auditor General. Unfortunately for Mackenzie, the country was in a state of depression when he took office. He had inherited a negative financial situation that could not be remedied during his term of office. Brown's mission to Washington was a failure and Mackenzie was forced to raise tariffs to raise money. This angered many people as Mackenzie had promised to lower tariffs. Others felt that he had not raised tariffs high enough on American goods so as to force Canadians to buy Canadian products.

In keeping with his working-class ideals, Mackenzie refused a knighthood from Queen Victoria on three occasions. His pride in his working-class origins never left him. He was a man of thoroughness and integrity, but he was hampered by a limited education. He tended to be stubborn and niaive. While holding both the positions of prime minister and minister of Public Works, he often spent up to fourteen hours a day on ministry business, neglecting the needs of other areas and the Liberal Party in general. In his own department, his honesty damaged his popularity because he refused to allow contractors to take their accustomed profits or to give contracts to Liberals. His amnesty to Louis Riel angered many English-speaking Canadians and his support of an act favouring prohibition angered many voters in Quebec. As a result, the Conservatives under Sir John A. Macdonald were returned to power in the election of 1878. He stayed on as leader of the Opposition for another two years.

Shortly after resigning as leader of the Liberal Party, Mackenzie suffered a paralyzing stroke. However, he still remained in politics as the member of Parliament for Lambton and in the 1882 election as the member for York East. In 1882, he published *The Life and Speeches of George Brown*. Although he was the director of several insurance companies, he was a poor man and depended on his parliamentary salary. He died on April 17, 1892, at his home in Toronto at the age of 70, still representing the electoral riding of York East.

The Prime Ministers of Canada　　　　　　　　　　　　　　　　　　Alexander MacKenzie

Name _____　　　**Date** _____

Points to Ponder

1. Why did Alexander Mackenzie come to Canada?
   _____
   _____
   _____

2. Name some of the structures that Mackenzie built that are still standing today.
   _____
   _____
   _____

3. What important accomplishments did Mackenzie make as prime minister?
   _____
   _____
   _____

4. What personal characteristics of Alexander Mackenzie encouraged people to vote for him?
   _____
   _____
   _____

5. How did Mackenzie's honesty cause him to become unpopular?
   _____
   _____
   _____

 Explore History

1. What is an auditor general? What does this person do? Why do you think Alexander Mackenzie created such an office?

2. Research one of the structures that Mackenzie built. Draw a picture of it.

3. What is the Royal Military College? Why was it created?

The Prime Ministers of Canada

Sir John Joseph Caldwell Abbott (1821 - 1893)
Prime Minister: 1891 - 1893

John Joseph Caldwell Abbott was born March 12, 1821, in St. Andrews East, Lower Canada. He was educated by his father, an Anglican missionary. At the age of seventeen he went to work in a dry goods business where he learned accounting and bookkeeping. In 1843, he started law school at the University of McGill College and joined the law firm of William Badgley when he was called to the bar in 1847. In 1849, he married Mary Bethune and they had eight children: four girls and four boys. One of his descendants is the actor, Christopher Plummer.

As a lawyer, Abbott became a recognized authority on commercial law, was appointed to the Queen's Counsel in 1862 and built a flourishing practice. He was a law professor at McGill University from 1853 to 1876 and Dean of Law from 1855 to 1880. He was a close associate of Sir Hugh Allan, one of the first promoters of the Canadian Pacific Railway. It was actually from Abbott's office that the papers which started the Pacific Scandal were stolen by a clerk. These documents revealed Allan's contributions to the Conservative Party at a time when he was negotiating for a contract to build the railway. When the company was reformed in 1880, Abbott was its solicitor and in 1887, he became a director.

Abbott also had another experience that his opponents did not let him forget. He signed the Annexation Manifesto of 1849 which advised that the British North American colonies give up their connection with Britain and join the United States. This resulted in Britain removing all preferential tariffs on products from Canada. Even though he had supported the policy, he later regretted the decision.

Abbott's political career began in 1857 when he stood for election as a Liberal for the constituency of Argenteuil to the Legislative Assembly of the Province of Canada. The election was disputed and it was two years before Abbott was declared elected. In 1862, he served as Attorney General in the government of John A. Macdonald and L.V. Sicotte. In 1865, he switched his allegiance from the Liberals to the Conservatives to support Confederation, and in 1867 he was elected to the House of Commons as the representative for his constituency. He was defeated in 1873 as a result of the Pacific Scandal, but was re-elected in 1881. He held this seat until 1887. In that year he was appointed to the Senate as a representative for the Inkerman division of Quebec and also served as a minister without portfolio in Sir John A. Macdonald's government. He was also government leader in the Senate as well as mayor of Montreal from 1887 to 1889.

The Prime Ministers of Canada

Abbott as Prime Minister

When Sir John A. Macdonald died in 1891, the government was left without a leader. The logical successor to Macdonald, John Thompson, was disqualified from taking the position because he had become a Roman Catholic. Abbott had to step in as prime minister even though he didn't want the job. He was the first prime minister to be appointed from the Senate and he did not hold a seat in the House of Commons. He was also the first prime minister to be born in Canada. One of his famous quotes about politics is: "I hate politics and what are considered appropriate methods. I hate notoriety, public meetings, public speeches, caucuses, and everything that I know of that is apparently the necessary incident of politics – except doing public work to the best of my ability." This was an unusual sentiment for a man who was to be the leader of the country.

During his short term of office he redistributed the parliamentary seats, reorganized the departments of Customs and Inland Revenue, reducing their ministers to non-Cabinet rank and created a new Department of Trade and Commerce. He revised the criminal code and signed a Reciprocity Treaty with the United States which allowed some manufactured goods to enter Canada free of charge. The Alaska boundary dispute was submitted to arbitration and plans were made to settle the Bering Sea Sealing dispute. He was unsuccessful in his attempts to bring Newfoundland into Confederation.

In November, 1892, Abbott was advised by his doctors to retire from politics. He recommended that John Thompson be appointed as his successor. He lived quietly for eleven months after his retirement and died on October 30, 1893, in Montreal, Quebec.

The Prime Ministers of Canada *Sir John Joseph Caldwell Abbott*

Name _____ **Date** _____

Points to Ponder

1. What were two ways Sir John Joseph Caldwell Abbott was different from the two prime ministers before him?

2. What did he accomplish during his short term in office?

3. How was he involved in the Pacific Scandal?

4. Why did Prime Minister Abbott switch from being a Liberal to being a Conservative?

5. What was the Annexation Manifesto? How did it affect Abbott?

🍁🍁 Explore History 🍁🍁

1. Sir Hugh Allan was a close friend of Prime Minister Abbott. Research Allan and why he was important in Canadian history.

2. How would you feel if you were a person who had voted for Sir John Joseph Caldwell Abbott after hearing the statement he made about politics? What do you think you might have done about it?

The Prime Ministers of Canada

Sir John Sparrow David Thompson (1845 - 1894)
Prime Minister: 1892 - 1894

John Sparrow David Thompson was born in Halifax, Nova Scotia, on November 10, 1845, the son of an Irish immigrant. He was educated at public elementary schools and at the Free Church Academy in Halifax. From the beginning, Thompson was a great debater and was articled to a Halifax lawyer at the age of fifteen. While studying law, he also learned shorthand and was appointed reporter at the provincial House of Assembly. After he was called to the Nova Scotia bar in 1865, he opened his own law office. He continued the job of reporting and in 1867, he was appointed chief reporter in the Assembly. These duties gave him a first hand knowledge of politics and he made many friends in the political field.

In 1870, Thompson married Anne Affleck of Halifax and they had two sons and three daughters. His wife was Roman Catholic and in 1871, Thompson himself became a Catholic. He was afraid that this conversion might affect his law practice, but instead it gave him his first start in politics.

In 1877, the Roman Catholic bishop convinced him to run for election in the by-election for the provincial legislature in the riding of Antigonish. The bishop had considerable influence and he helped Thompson win the election. He continued to work as a lawyer gaining fame for assisting the United States in preparing a case against the Halifax Fisheries Commission. Even though he was criticized for this action, he gained valuable knowledge for his later political career.

In 1878, he was appointed Attorney General in the Conservative government of Simon Holmes. In this position, he helped pass the bill to aid the School of Law at Dalhousie University and he was also the lawyer in many criminal cases. When Holmes resigned, Thompson became premier of Nova Scotia but was defeated in an election a few months later. He then became a justice of the provincial Supreme Court. While in this position, he drafted the Nova Scotia Judicature Act of 1884 and gave a series of lectures on evidence at the Dalhousie Law School.

The turning point in his career came in 1885, when he was approached by Sir John A. Macdonald to run for a federal seat in the riding of Antigonish. He won the seat and was tested by Louis Riel in the Red River Rebellion. It was Thompson that sentenced Riel to death for treason and refused to commute the sentence. He defended his position in Parliament with a powerful speech that even won over some of his opponents.

The Prime Ministers of Canada

In 1885, he was part of a group that was sent to Washington to negotiate a fishing treaty with the United States. Although the United States refused to adopt the treaty, Thompson was knighted for the part he played. In 1888, he was involved in disallowing the Jesuit Estates Act to be passed in the House of Commons, which would have compensated the Jesuits for large tracts of land in Quebec that had been taken over by the government.

Thompson was the logical successor to Sir John A. Macdonald, but he had made many enemies in Ontario and Quebec and so John Abbott was appointed to the position of prime minister instead. However, it was Thompson who performed most of the prime minister's duties during this time. He remained as Minister of Justice and drafted a new Criminal Code of Canada which was passed in 1892.

Thompson as Prime Minister

When Thompson took office as Prime Minister on December 5, 1892, he did not make any radical changes to the government. He increased the size of Cabinet, but did not dismiss any ministers. Much of his time as prime minister was spent abroad attending conferences in England and France. He promised to reform tariffs, but avoided any major controversies. He rarely spoke during the 1894 sitting of the Parliament. The most pressing issue he faced as prime minister was the Manitoba Schools Question and he avoided this issue by referring it to the courts.

On December 12, 1894, he attended a ceremony at Windsor Castle in London, England where he was sworn into the Privy Council. During the ceremony, he died of a heart attack.

The Prime Ministers of Canada   *Sir John Sparrow David Thompson*

Name _____ **Date** _____

Points to Ponder

1. How did Thompson's early experience as a reporter for the government help him later on in his career?
   _____
   _____

2. How did Thompson get his first real start in politics?
   _____
   _____

3. How did Thompson become involved in federal politics?
   _____
   _____

4. What were his political accomplishments?
   _____
   _____
   _____
   _____

5. Do you think Thompson was effective as a prime minister? Why or why not?
   _____
   _____
   _____
   _____

 Explore History

1. What was the Manitoba Schools Question? Why was it important in Canadian history?

2. What was the Bering Sea Sealing issue?

3. What changes did Thompson make to the Criminal Code of Canada?

The Prime Ministers of Canada

MacKenzie Bowell (1823 - 1917)
Prime Minister: 1894 - 1896

Mackenzie Bowell was born on December 27, 1823, in Rickinghall, England, the son of a carpenter and builder. The family emigrated to Upper Canada in 1833 and settled in Belleville. At the age of eleven, Bowell was apprenticed to the printer of the local newspaper, *The Intelligencer*, where he remained, eventually becoming the editor and later the owner of the newspaper. He joined the Orange Association of British North America which was the main instrument of the Conservative party at the time. He rose to become leader of the association and had considerable political influence. He married Harriet Moore in 1847 and they had nine children. He joined the local militia, served with it during the Fenian Raids and became lieutenant-colonel. He remained with the militia until 1874.

In 1867, he was elected to the first Canadian House of Commons to represent the riding of North Hastings and retained that seat throughout the following six elections. His hometown of Belleville was a growing manufacturing town, so Bowell was in favour of protective tariffs. In the election of 1878, he became Minister of Customs and was able to put the National Policy of Sir John A. Macdonald into operation which included protective tariffs. He kept the portfolio of Customs for thirteen years until 1892, when under the administration of Sir John Abbott, he became Minister of Militia and Defense, moving to Minister of Trade and Commerce under Sir John Thompson. In 1892, he was also appointed to the Senate.

As Minister of Trade and Commerce he advocated protective tariffs. He thought of commercial union with the United States as treason. He was responsible for delegating to Australia the first paid trade commissioner ever sent abroad by Canada. The Intercolonial Trade Conference of 1894 was the central event of his time as minister. He prepared the work for the conference and stated Canada's position quite clearly: if Canada was to prefer British goods over American, then Britain should prefer Canadian goods over those of other countries.

Bowell as Prime Minister

When Sir John Thompson died in December 1894, Bowell became the acting prime minister. He was the oldest man in Parliament and had a longer political career than most of the other members. He was 70 years old and was too old to do a good job. The written records of many committee meetings were lost and the Cabinet was often argumentative. Some Cabinet ministers resigned over his handling of the Manitoba Schools. He resigned as prime minister in 1896. He was the second and last prime minister to also be a member of the Senate. He died on December 10, 1917.

The Prime Ministers of Canada *Mackenzie Bowell*

Name _____   **Date** _____

Points to Ponder

1. Why do you think Mackenzie Bowell was re-elected to represent the constituency of North Hastings so often?
   _____
   _____
   _____

2. Why was Bowell in favour of having protective tariffs on Canadian goods?
   _____
   _____
   _____

3. What was Canada's position on trade with Britain at the Intercolonial Conference?
   _____
   _____
   _____

4. What qualities prevented Bowell from being an efficient prime minister?
   _____
   _____
   _____
   _____

 Explore History

1. Bowell took part in the Fenian Raids. Research this event in Canadian history and write a report about it.

2. What was the importance of protective tarrifs?

3. Bowell considered commercial union with the United States a form of "treason." What is treason?

The Prime Ministers of Canada

Sir Charles Tupper (1821 - 1915)
Prime Minister: 1896 - 1896

Charles Tupper was born on July 2, 1821, in Halifax, Nova Scotia. He was educated at Horton Academy (now Acadia University), Wolfeville and completed his medical training in 1843 at the University of Edinburgh, Scotland. He married Frances Morse in 1846 and they had six children. He successfully practiced medicine in Amherst for several years before entering politics in 1855, when he was 34 years old. Through his practice, he had developed a large number of influential friends who helped him defeat prominent politician, Joseph Howe, for the Cumberland seat in the Legislative Assembly. He became premier of Nova Scotia in 1863. His leadership in Nova Scotia was marked by a reorganization of the province's education system.

Tupper supported responsible government and also favoured a union of the four Atlantic colonies. He organized a conference on the issue to take place in Charlottetown, Prince Edward Island, in 1864. John A. Macdonald and Georges-Etienne Cartier requested permission to attend, bringing with them the idea of a Canadian Union. It is because of this that Tupper is known as one of the Fathers of Confederation. When Confederation became a reality in 1867, he did not take a seat in the new Cabinet, stepping aside instead to allow a fair representation of Roman Catholics and Protestants. He became a member of the Council in 1870 under the leadership of Sir. John A. Macdonald. During these years, he succeeded in convincing Joseph Howe to support Confederation and even encouraged him to take part in the Macdonald government.

In 1872, Tupper was made Minister of Inland Revenue and he was Minister of Customs when the Pacific Scandal forced Macdonald to resign in 1873. After the election of 1874, Tupper was one of the few Conservatives to be re-elected. When Macdonald was returned to power in 1878, Tupper was appointed Minister of Public Works. He improved the Intercolonial Railway and introduced legislation creating the Canadian Pacific Railway. When the railway almost went bankrupt in 1884, he pushed through a bill which authorized more money for its completion.

In 1884, Tupper became the Canadian High Commissioner to London and returned to Canada in 1887 to become Minister of Finance. He was a likely successor to Macdonald after his death, but chose instead to stay in London. He returned to Canada after the resignation of Mackenzie Bowell to take over the post of prime minister. However, the five year term was up and he had to call an election after only 69 days in office. The Conservatives lost the election, but Tupper remained as Conservative leader until 1901. That year he retired from politics and returned to England, where he died on October 30, 1915. He has the distinction of having had the shortest term of any Canadian prime minister.

The Prime Ministers of Canada   Sir Charles Tupper

Name _____ Date _____

Points to Ponder

1. How did Tupper's medical career help his political career?
   _____
   _____

2. What was one major thing he accomplished as premier of Nova Scotia?
   _____
   _____

3. What was the original intention of the Charlottetown Conference?
   _____
   _____

4. Why didn't Tupper have a Cabinet post in 1867?
   _____
   _____

5. Why didn't he accept the position of prime minister in 1891?
   _____
   _____

6. Why did he call an election immediately after becoming prime minister?
   _____
   _____

 Explore History

1. Research the following terms and write a short note on each one:
   a) the Charlottetown Conference
   b) the Quebec Conference
   c) the London Conference
   d) Intercolonial Railway

2. What is the office of the High Commissioner? What does this office do?

The Prime Ministers of Canada

Sir Wilfrid Laurier (1841 - 1919)
Prime Minister: 1896 - 1911

Wilfrid Laurier was born on November 20, 1841, in St. Lin (now Laurentides), Lower Canada. His mother died when he was only four years old and he was raised by a stepmother. He was sent to a Protestant school in New Glasgow, where he lived with an Irish family and learned to speak fluent English. He then attended L'Assumption College and went on to study law at McGill University. While he was at university, he entered the law offices of Rodolphe Laflamme, one of the leaders of the Parti Rouge, one of the most liberal factions in Quebec. He also joined the Institut Canadien, a literary and scientific society that attracted many young liberals, radicals and anti-clerics. Both these groups were under attack by the Roman Catholic Church and although Laurier was a devout Catholic, he defended his right to hold political beliefs not endorsed by the Church. Because of the stand that he took on this issue, the clergy was opposed to him entering politics.

After studying and practicing law in Montreal, Laurier opened a law office in L'Avenir in 1866 and later moved to Victoriaville. Here he also became a journalist for *Le Defricheur*. This radical weekly paper vigorously opposed Confederation and the social and political domination of the Catholic clergy. He moved to Arthabaskaville, now Arthabaska, in 1867. This move began his political career.

In 1871, Laurier won the seat for Arthabaska for the Quebec provincial legislature, but resigned this seat in 1874 to run for the federal seat of Arthabaska and Drummond. His first important speech in the House of Commons glorified the British Empire. In it he stressed that his liberalism was of the moderate British type, not the anti-clerical type of European countries which had been denounced by the Pope. This opened the way for Catholics to vote for him with a clear conscience.

By 1877, he had already proven himself as one of the most promising young men supporting the Liberal party. He was chosen to be Minister of Inland Revenue, but by Canadian law, a newly appointed minister had to stand for re-election. Due to a campaign against him by the Catholic clergy, some even saying that it would be a sin to vote for him, Laurier lost the election by 29 votes. The party thought he was too valuable a member to lose, so a Quebec East member was persuaded to resign and allow Laurier to run for election in his seat. He won the by-election and continued to hold this seat for 40 years.

The Prime Ministers of Canada

He did not enjoy his position for very long as Macdonald's Conservatives were returned to power in 1878. Laurier continued to build a personal following in Quebec and in the election of 1882, he not only won the seat but accepted the position of mayor of Arthabaska. During the Red River Rebellion, Laurier sympathized with the plight of Louis Riel and denounced the government in Parliament and at a public meeting in Montreal.

Laurier became leader of the Liberal Party in 1888 after the resignation of Edward Blake. This was the first time the Party had been led by a French Canadian. In the 1896 election, the Manitoba Schools Question was a major issue. Laurier argued that he would obtain better terms for the Catholics in Manitoba by negotiating directly with the provincial government. "Hands Off Manitoba" became the slogan of his campaign. A second controversial issue was the corruption in the Conservative Party. Israel Tarte, a former Quebec Conservative who had evidence of this corruption, managed Laurier's campaign and as a result the Liberals were returned to power. Laurier became Prime Minister of Canada on July 11, 1896 making Laurier the first French Canadian prime minister.

Laurier as Prime Minister

The first task facing the new government was to try to solve the Manitoba Schools Question. Laurier pushed through a plan that would allow a limited amount of religious teaching and instruction in the French language schools in Manitoba. However, it did not return the education of the province to its former system of equality between Catholics and Protestants. This handling of the issue angered Roman Catholic clergy in Quebec and the Pope had to step in to end their political domination by restraining the bishops.

Laurier's first budget was a compromise between his declared free trade views and the need to protect Canadian industries. He made only a slight reduction in the tariffs and offered Britain imperial preference on all its trade with Canada. This made Laurier a key figure at the Colonial Trade Conference in 1897. At this time, he was also knighted by Queen Victoria and received the Legion d'Honneur from the president of France.

When the Boer War broke out in 1899, Britain believed that it should be wholeheartedly supported by Canada. However, French Canadians believed that this issue had nothing to do with Canada. Again Laurier compromised, sending a contingent of volunteers. This did not adequately satisfy either side, but the Liberals were returned to power in 1900.

The Prime Ministers of Canada

Laurier reaffirmed Canada's position and refused to cooperate in a common defence policy at the Colonial Trade Conference of 1902. At this time he became ill and offered to resign. However, the party members refused to accept his resignation. Two setbacks affected the government in 1903: the Alaska Boundary Dispute and the resignation of the minister of Railways. In the dispute with the United States over the Alaska boundary, the British representative sided with the United States and infuriated Laurier over what he called the lack of the Canadian government's power to deal with its own problems. His minister of Railways resigned over Laurier's decision to build a second transcontinental railway to compete with the one built by the Conservatives. The railway line was built at enormous cost to Canadian taxpayers and a third line was built in 1911.

Yukon Territory was created under the Laurier administration in 1898 with Dawson as its capital and the provinces of Alberta and Saskatchewan were created in 1905. Another schools question ensued in the Northwest Territories and Laurier attempted to follow the system which had been set up in Ontario. This system had separate Roman Catholic schools supported through taxes. This time the objections came from the Protestants. Eventually a compromise was worked out.

In 1900, Laurier created the Department of Labour and in 1909, the Department of External Affairs. That same year, Britain called upon Canada to define its naval policy. Ontario wanted Canada to contribute to the British navy, but Quebec would have no part of it. Laurier again compromised by proposing the creation of a Canadian navy to be built and trained in accordance with British naval requirements and placed under British command if Canada ever chose to enter a war with Britain. The Naval Service Bill of 1910 which created the Royal Canadian Navy was a compromise which was not satisfactory to either side. The Conservatives believed that Canada should just provide ships for the British navy, while Quebec nationalists did not want Canada to participate in any way. In 1911, Laurier worked out a Reciprocity Agreement on tariffs with the United States. The terms of this agreement were highly favourable to Canada, but railway interests were not included in the agreement and an election held on the issue saw the defeat of the Liberal government.

Laurier remained leader of the Opposition and refused to compromise with the onservatives over the conscription issue in 1917. This issue also split the Liberal Party. It seemed that the only ones who opposed conscription were French Canadians. It also seemed that Laurier's party was purely French Canadian and his vision of Canada united through compromise had not succeeded. He died February 17, 1919.

The Prime Ministers of Canada   *Sir Wilfrid Laurier*

Name _____   **Date** _____

Points to Ponder

1. Why was the Roman Catholic clergy opposed to Wilfrid Laurier?
   _____
   _____

2. What did he do to win Catholic votes when he was elected to Parliament?
   _____
   _____

3. How did Laurier handle the Manitoba Schools Question?
   _____
   _____

4. How did Laurier become important at the Colonial Trade Conferences?
   _____
   _____

5. Why was he angered by the British handling of the Alaska Boundary Dispute?
   _____
   _____

6. What were some of the accomplishments of his term as Prime Minister?
   _____
   _____

 Explore History

1. What was the Alaska Boundary Dispute? Draw a map showing the boundaries that Canada wanted. How do they differ from the boundaries today?

2. How did Laurier settle the issue of separate schools in the Northwest Territories?

3. Why did French Canadians oppose conscription?

The Prime Ministers of Canada

Sir Robert Laird Borden (1854 - 1937)
Prime Minister: 1911 - 1920

Robert Laird Borden was born on June 26, 1854, in Grand Pré, Nova Scotia. He did not attend school regularly when he was younger as he was needed to work on the family farm. He studied at home and also at the Villa Seminary in Horton, Nova Scotia. At the age of fourteen, he was a teacher at the school. At age nineteen, he was apprenticed to a law firm in Halifax and was called to the bar in 1878. He opened his own law office in Kentville and in 1882, he was invited to become a junior partner of one of the largest law firms in Halifax. In 1889, he married Laura Bond and although the marriage was a happy one, they did not have any children. In 1890, he became the senior partner of his law firm; in 1891, he was appointed to the Queen's Counsel.

In 1896, he was persuaded by Sir Charles Tupper to run for election as a Conservative in one of Halifax's two federal seats. Even though the Tupper government was defeated, Borden won his seat and went to Parliament as a member of the Opposition. He did not like the lack of rational debate, the hypocrisy and the politicking he found in Parliament. His first speech attacked the spoils system, which he believed to be the cause of inefficiency and corruption in government. However, this system was favoured by his own party. When Sir Charles Tupper resigned as party leader in 1900, Borden was offered the position. He did not want it, but accepted it out of a sense of duty in 1901, and gave up practicing law.

He was defeated in the election of 1904, but successfully ran in the by-election in 1905 for the seat of Carleton. He also moved to Ottawa, so he could give more attention to his duties. In 1906, he reorganized the Conservative Party, determined to impose some sort of unity. However, he lost some of his party's support in 1907, when he set forth the Halifax Manifesto which proposed: reform of the Senate, stricter supervision of immigration, nationalization of the telephone and telegraph systems, a commission to regulate public utilities, a protective tariff, and government control of the resources of the west. In the election of 1911, Borden campaigned against the Reciprocity Treaty signed by Sir Wilfrid Laurier, claiming it was the first step to Canada becoming part of the United States. The Conservatives were returned to power and Borden became Prime Minister of Canada on October 10, 1911.

The Prime Ministers of Canada

Borden as Prime Minister

Borden continued some of the policies which had been in place under the Liberals, such as those on immigration, and even the transcontinental railway, which he had opposed while in opposition. This showed that he was committed to the task of nation-building in Canada. However, he made no attempt to implement the Naval Service Bill of 1910 and instead tried to draft his own Naval Aid Bill which would see Canada purchasing three ships for the British navy in return for a greater say in imperial policy. He was bombarded by letters from Winston Churchill who said the idea of a Canadian navy was foolish. After a week of 24 hour debates on the issue, he pushed the bill through the House of Commons. However, it was not passed in the Senate and he allowed the issue to drop.

When the First World War broke out in 1914, even the French Canadians were in favour of Canada going to war. A War Measures Act was passed in 1914 that put most of the power of Parliament into the hands of the Cabinet. Under this act, the government could censure the media, arrest people on suspicion, imprison people without trial, and control communications and transportation. Thousands of Canadians volunteered and Borden raised money to support the war effort by taxing the profits of companies that made war supplies. Borden became disillusioned with the lack of British concern about the war, and threatened to withdraw Canadian troops if there was not more cooperation between Britain and Canada about the war effort.

In 1916, the Ontario government passed a law making English the first language of the province. This angered Quebecers, but Borden did not take any action. The passing of the Military Voters' Act and the War Time Election Act also made enemies for Borden, as these measures took the right to vote away from conscientious objectors to the war and anyone who spoke German. In the same year, he brought in Canada's first income tax. This was supposed to be temporary but it became permanent.

Up to 1917, all of the Canadian forces who fought in the First World War were volunteers. The Military Service Act of 1917 brought conscription to Canada. This was bitterly resented by the French Canadians, and discontent spread throughout the country. In 1919, Borden established the Employment Services of Canada which was designed to help people find jobs.

After the war, Borden served as Canada's chief representative at the peace talks in Paris. He insisted that the peace treaties be signed separately by Canada. This was the first time that Canada was recognized internationally as an independent country. He encouraged the other countries to form a League of Nations to prevent the outbreak of another world war, and insisted that Canada be a member of the League.

When he returned to Canada, he embarked on many speaking tours to restore voters' faith in the Conservative Party. He resigned from office due to ill health on July 10, 1920. He regained his health and represented Great Britain at the Washington Conference in 1921. He represented Canada at the League of Nations and was Canada's chief delegate in 1930. He was chancellor of McGill University from 1918 - 1920 and Queen's University from 1924 - 1930. He died at Ottawa on June 10, 1937.

The Prime Ministers of Canada   *Sir Robert Laird Borden*

Name _____ Date _____

Points to Ponder

1. What did Borden dislike about Parliament? What did he do about it?
   _____
   _____

2. How did Borden show that he took his political job seriously?
   _____
   _____

3. What was the Halifax Manifesto?
   _____
   _____
   _____

4. Why do you think Borden continued many Liberal policies after he became prime minister?
   _____
   _____
   _____

5. What powers did the War Measures Act give Parliament?
   _____
   _____
   _____

6. How did Borden gain international recognition for Canada?
   _____
   _____

 Explore History

1. What was the League of Nations? What countries were members of this League?

2. What is income tax? Why is it necessary?

3. What is conscription? Why were so many Canadians opposed to the idea of conscription?

The Prime Ministers of Canada

Arthur Meighen (1874 - 1960)
Prime Minister: 1920 - 1921
June 29, 1926 - September 25, 1926

Arthur Meighen was born on June 16, 1874 on a farm near St. Mary's, Ontario. He received his early education at St. Mary's Collegiate and later graduated from the University of Toronto where he studied mathematics. He taught at a nearby college institute, and then decided to borrow money to start his own business. The business failed and he returned to teaching at a high school in Caledonia, Ontario. He then decided to go into law, and in 1903, he opened his own law office in Portage la Prairie, Manitoba where he soon gained a reputation as a brilliant prosecuting attorney. In 1904 he married Isabel Cox. They had three children: two sons and one daughter. In 1908, he ran as the local Conservative candidate in the federal election and won what had been known as a safe Liberal seat. This marked the beginning of his political career. He easily made his presence known in Parliament with his inventive and often scathing wit. His rise within the ranks of the Conservative Party over the next few years was phenomenal. He loved to debate and was very good at it.

In 1913, during the administration of Sir Robert Borden, Meighen was appointed to the post of Solicitor General. Almost immediately he was involved in controversy. Borden tried to pass his own naval bill and the Opposition filibustered (staged a 24 hour debate for almost two weeks) until Meighen planned and put into effect a closure motion that pushed the bill through the House of Commons. However, the bill was not passed in the Senate. This matter gained Meighen a lot of enemies among those opposed to the bill.

In 1915, he gained a Cabinet seat as Solicitor General. He fully supported the war effort, even stating that he was willing to bankrupt Canada to help pay for it, and was one of the first Cabinet Ministers to support conscription. He introduced two bills before the election of 1917 to keep those opposed to conscription from voting: The Military Voters Act and the War Times Election Act. These measures allowed the female relatives of men on active service to vote, while disallowing those who objected to the war and German-speaking citizens of Canada. These bills were passed but they widened the cultural division between French and English-speaking Canadians. Meighen is also recognized as the author of the Military Service Act which introduced conscription and also as the member of Parliament who pushed it through. It further ensured that voters in Quebec would always vote against him.

In the election of 1917, Meighen was re-elected and was given the post of Minister of the Interior in a new coalition government under Borden. In this position, he had the government take over the Canadian Pacific, the Grand Trunk and the Canadian Northern Railways. The Canadian Northern Railway became bankrupt in 1917 and was taken over by the government. By 1919, the other railways were taken over and in 1923 Meighen succeeded in consolidating the railways into the Canadian National Railway. He was accused of speaking for railway promoters,

The Prime Ministers of Canada

and even though this was not true, Meighen became known as a friend of big business. During the Winnipeg General Strike, Meighen detected a Bolshevik conspiracy and urged the arrest and deportation of six of the strike leaders. There was also a bloody attack on the strikers by the police. When Borden retired in 1920, the Conservatives were forced to accept Meighen as Prime Minister in spite of the fact that voters disliked him.

Meighen as Prime Minister

Meighen became Prime Minister of Canada on July 10, 1920. For his first few months Meighen did not do any significant work in Canada. During the summer of 1921, he attended the Imperial Conference in Britain to discuss the renewal of the treaty between Great Britain and Japan. Meighen suggested a new treaty which would include all of the Pacific powers. In spite of opposition, Britain agreed and a new conference was held in Washington in December, 1921. Even though the new treaty had been Meighen's idea, the United States almost forgot to invite Canada to the conference.

It was time for a national election and Meighen waited as long as possible, until December 1921. Canada was going through a postwar depression and many people blamed the Conservative government for this. As a result, Meighen lost the election, and resigned as Prime Minister on December 29.

Meighen regained a seat in the House of Commons and was leader of the Opposition until 1926. That year the Conservatives discovered a scandal in the Customs Department that involved bootleg whiskey and cigarettes. Rather than call an election, Prime Minister William Lyon MacKenzie King resigned after asking Lord Byng, the Governor-General, to dissolve the Parliament. Meighen stepped in to become prime minister for a second time. He was certain that he would win the election on the Customs issue, but King claimed that Byng and Meighen had reverted Canada to a British colony. Meighen served a second term while he was campaigning for an election from July 29 to September 29, 1926.

Meighen retired from politics and began a successful business career in Toronto. In 1932, he accepted a seat in the Senate. In 1941, he was approached by the Conservatives to become the party leader and he agreed to give up his seat in the Senate. However, he was defeated in the ensuing by-election. This time, he retired from politics for good. He devoted the rest of his life to his business affairs. He died in Toronto on August 5, 1960.

The Prime Ministers of Canada   *Arthur Meighen*

Name _____ **Date** _____

Points to Ponder

1. What was the first controversy Meighen was involved in?
   _____
   _____

2. Why were the Military Voters Act and the War Times Election Act so unpopular?
   _____
   _____

3. What part did Meighen play in the Winnipeg General Strike?
   _____
   _____

4. How did Meighen change how railways were operated in Canada?
   _____
   _____

5. What part did he play in getting a treaty for all of the Pacific Rim countries?
   _____
   _____

 Explore History

1. The Opposition "filibustered" when the new Naval Bill was introduced. What does this mean? Does this type of behaviour still occur in the House of Commons today? Give an example.

2. What was the Winnipeg General Strike? Who were the key players and what did they want? How did it end?

3. Draw a map showing the routes followed by:
   a) the Canadian Pacific Railway
   b) the Grand Trunk Railway
   c) the Canadian Northern Railway

The Prime Ministers of Canada

William Lyon Mackenzie King (1874 - 1950)
Prime Minister: December 29, 1921- June 28, 1926
September 25, 1926 - August 7, 1930
October 23, 1935 - November 15, 1948

William Lyon Mackenzie King was born December 17, 1874, in Berlin (now Kitchener), Ontario. He was named for his grandfather William Lyon Mackenzie who led the Rebellion of 1837 in Upper Canada. He grew up hearing stories about his grandfather and took a keen interest in politics and economics. In 1891, he went to the University of Toronto to study law, but he later changed his mind and studied government and economics instead. He won a scholarship to the University of Chicago and did postgraduate studies at Harvard University.

While in Toronto and Chicago, King was appalled at the poverty he witnessed in these cities. He took a job as a reporter for the Toronto newspaper, *Mail and Empire,* during the summer of 1897 and made a study of the working conditions of the garment industry. He found that the factories making postmen's uniforms had some of the worst conditions. He relayed this information to the Postmaster General, Sir William Mulock, a friend of his, and suggested that any factory making the uniforms be forced in a contract to give fair wages to their employees. Mulock took his advice, and in 1900, he invited King to administer Canada's first Department of Labour. King accepted the position of Deputy Minister of Labour at age 25. For the next eight years, King remained in this position, working to improve labour conditions all over the country. He helped to settle strikes, drafted labour legislation and served on national and international committees. King also had to support his family during these years and so he never married.

In 1908, he won the seat of Waterloo North in the federal election and became Minister of Labour. He lost this seat in the election of 1911. He then worked in minor jobs within the Liberal Party, and in 1914 he accepted a job as director of industrial research with the Rockefeller Foundation in the United States. In 1918, he wrote *Industry and Humanity* which set out his beliefs about labour and capitalism. This book advocated cooperation between community, labour and industrial companies. It recommended a larger share of the control of capital for the state and represented a step toward a welfare state. However, this was as close as King ever came to formulating a political creed and it made little impression on his colleagues.

The Prime Ministers of Canada

He was re-elected at the age of 45 to Parliament representing Prince, Prince Edward Island in 1919. He was also elected leader of the Liberal Party. Some people opposed this because he had not fought in the First World War. He made a great speech in Parliament defending his reasons stating that he had to remain home to support his family. In the election of 1921, King and the Liberals were two seats short of a majority. The Progressive Party agreed to vote with him, but refused to join the Liberal Party or act as the official Opposition.

King as Prime Minister

During the first few years of his first term, King did not initiate any new policies. He basically left ministers to their own affairs as long as they did not embarrass the government. He set about reorganizing the Party, corresponding regularly with local workers and taking an interest in the smallest details of patronage. He also left Quebec politics in the hands of Ernest Lapointe, his second-in-command.

King was very careful to avoid controversial issues. In 1922, when Britain requested Canadian support in a threatened war against Turkey, he refused to commit Canada without getting the approval of Parliament. The next year, Britain tried to set up a common foreign policy for all parts of its empire and King refused to cooperate. By standing firm against this action, he ensured that the Commonwealth would consist of independent nations.

King and the Liberals lost the election of 1925, but uncovered a Customs scandal. In the election which followed in 1926, the Liberals won and King had a second term as prime minister. During the next few years he had few problems, but was unable to prevent a depression in 1930 and did little to relieve it. As a result he was defeated in the election of 1930.

While in Opposition, King suggested the establishment of a central bank controlled by the government to try to deal with the depression. In the 1935 election, the Liberals ran on a platform based on the idea that the Conservatives had stolen their ideas for reform. Again, he was reinstated as prime minister of Canada. His first act was to reduce the trade barriers between Canada and the United States, followed by a reduction of tariffs with Great Britain. He advocated a spirit of cooperation between nations, and when the Canadian representative at the League of Nations suggested tough measures against Italy for its war on Ethiopia, King recalled him back to Canada. This action helped to bring about the end of the League of Nations.

The Prime Ministers of Canada

In 1937, King met with Adolf Hitler and characterized him as "a simple little peasant." King kept Canada's military expenditures to a minimum. He continued to hope in appeasing Hitler until after the Munich Pact. When it became clear in 1939 that there would be another world war, he remembered the problems of the First World War and began a long struggle to preserve the unity of Canada. He pledged Canada's support to Great Britain, but also assured the French Canadians that there would be no conscription. When war did break out on September 1, 1939, King dissolved Parliament on September 7 because of problems which had arisen in Quebec and Ontario. His government subsequently won a substantial majority in Parliament.

Conscription was introduced during the war, but only for an army that would stay home for defence. King became an intermediary between Winston Churchill, the British Prime Minister, and Franklin D. Roosevelt, the President of the United States. He helped the United States to set up military bases in Newfoundland in return for naval ships. Because of this assistance, he had little trouble in working with Roosevelt in 1941 on an integrated plan for war production – the Hyde Park Declaration. This also helped Canada to avoid bankruptcy.

King appointed the first woman, Carine Wilson, to the Senate in 1930. He brought in unemployment insurance in 1940 and the family allowance in 1944. King again won an election in 1945. In 1947, he was admitted to the Order of Merit, the first Canadian to gain membership. He resigned as prime minister on November 15, 1948, holding office longer than any other prime minister. He died in Kingsmere, Quebec, in 1950.

The Prime Ministers of Canada — *William Lyon Mackenzie King*

Name _____ Date _____

Points to Ponder

1. How did King obtain the position of Deputy Minister of Labour?
   _____
   _____
   _____

2. What did he write about in his book *Industry and Humanity*?
   _____
   _____

3. What did King do to avoid controversial issues? Give an example.
   _____
   _____

4. How did he manage to please the people of Quebec over the conscription issue?
   _____
   _____

5. What did he do to ensure that Canada had a place in world politics?
   _____
   _____

 Explore History

1. What was King's description of Hitler? Was he correct in this assessment? Why or why not?

2. What was the Munich Pact? Why did King think it would avert a war?

3. Research the King-Byng Affair. How did it affect King's administration?

4. King brought in the policy of old-age pensions. What was the amount given to senior citizens at this time? How has it changed?

The Prime Ministers of Canada

Richard Bedford Bennett (1870 - 1947)
Prime Minister: 1930 - 1935

Richard Bedford Bennett was born on July 3, 1870, in Hopewell Hill, New Brunswick. His father was a shipbuilder at a time when the industry was declining, so he grew up in an atmosphere that emphasized economy, industry and piety. He taught school until 1890, and then began to study law with L.J. Tweedie in Chatham, New Brunswick. After graduating from Dalhousie in 1893, he joined the Tweedie firm as a junior partner. Tweedie became premier of New Brunswick, giving Bennett his first introduction to politics. In 1896, he was elected to Chatham's town council. Bennett then moved to Calgary in 1897 becoming junior partner to another Conservative, J.A. Lougheed. In 1898, he was elected to the legislature of the Northwest Territories and in 1911 to the House of Commons in Ottawa, representing Calgary West. Bennett was a highly successful businessman, as he became the director of two of Lord Beaverbrook's companies, and opened his own law office in 1922. In 1923, he became a director of the Royal Bank of Canada and in 1926, he gained control of a pulp and paper company.

As a member of Parliament, Bennett was a confirmed prohibitionist and bitterly opposed separate Roman Catholic schools in the Prairie provinces. He criticized the settlement, land-granting and immigration policies of the government and wanted to see the governments railway policies change. He thought that the new railway systems were unnecessary and the contribution of funds extravagant. He found his first experience in federal politics discouraging and often was opposed to his own party's policies. During the First World War, he was appointed to the position of Director General of National Service. He believed that conscription to military service should be introduced, but the bill was defeated by the coalition government. As a result of his objections to the coalition, he was not invited to become a member of the reorganized Cabinet. He decided not to run in the election of 1917, predicting that within 25 years Canada would become part of the United States. He thought about moving into British politics, but decided to retire instead.

He was re-elected in 1925 and also elected to succeed Meighen as leader of the Conservative party in 1927. He was the first party leader in Canada to be elected in a Leadership Convention. In his campaign of 1930, he promised to build new branches of the railway, a St. Lawrence waterway, and to pay full cost of old-age pensions. His government won the election and on August 7, 1930, he became prime minister.

The Prime Ministers of Canada

Bennett as Prime Minister

Within a month of becoming prime minister, Bennett obtained an increase in tariffs and a grant of twenty million dollars for unemployment insurance for one winter. He was the first prime minister to make full use of the civil service; he used personnel from various departments to draft legislation, negotiate trade agreements or to act as economic advisors. In 1931, he accepted the Statute of Westminster, which gave Canada the power to amend its own constitution. He also negotiated the St. Lawrence Deep Waterways Treaty with the United States in 1932. His government created the Canadian Broadcasting Corporation (CBC) in 1932 and established the Bank of Canada in 1935. He lost the election of 1935, but remained in politics until 1938. He died in 1947 in Surrey, England, and is the only Canadian prime minister to be buried outside the country.

The Prime Ministers of Canada *Richard Bedford Bennett*

Name _____ **Date** _____

Points to Ponder

1. Do you think Bennett was popular in Quebec? Why or why not?
   _____
   _____
   _____
   _____

2. What are two "firsts" that Bennett is noted for?
   _____
   _____

3. What are some of the accomplishments of his administration?
   _____
   _____
   _____

4. Why do you think his campaign promises helped him win the election of 1930?
   _____
   _____

5. How did he utilize the civil service?
   _____
   _____

 Explore History

1. What was the Statue of Westminster? How did it benefit Canada?

2. How were Conservative party leaders chosen before Bennett? Do you think this was a better practice? Why or why not?

3. During the 1930s many people in Canada were said to be "on the dole." What does this mean? Where does the phrase come from?

The Prime Ministers of Canada

Louis Stephen St. Laurent (1882 - 1973)
Prime Minister: 1948 - 1957

Louis Stephen St. Laurent was born February 1, 1882, in Compden, Quebec, the son of a French-speaking storekeeper and an English-speaking teacher. He was a child of two cultures and fluent in both English and French. He became a lawyer and established a successful practice. He married Jeanne Renault in 1908 and they had five children. He had no desire to enter politics, and it was not until 1941 that he was approached by William Lyon Mackenzie King to come to Ottawa. King's second-in-command Ernest Lapointe had died and King needed a person to handle Quebec politics. St. Laurent was 59 years old at the time, but he agreed, feeling that it was his duty to Canada to take on the job.

In 1942, he was elected to the House of Commons as the member of Parliament for Quebec East. He was appointed Justice Minister and played an important role in helping King win acceptance in Canada for a conscription policy. He planned to quit politics after the Second World War was over. However, King persuaded him to stay and appointed him Minister of External Affairs. St. Laurent emerged as the most important advisor in the Cabinet. As Attorney General in 1945 to 1946, he played a major role in dealing with an elaborate spy network which was allegedly passing Canadian nuclear secrets to the Soviets. When King retired in 1948, the party chose St. Laurent to be their leader at the age of 66. He became prime minister of Canada on November 15, 1948.

St. Laurent as Prime Minister

St. Laurent was a very friendly and modest person. The newspapers at the time nicknamed him " Uncle Louis." Because the Canadian economy was healthy, the St. Laurent government was able to expand the social welfare measures begun by King. His foreign policy involved Canada in world politics. He supported the United Nations and cooperated with North Atlantic Treaty Organization (NATO), even formulating an expanding economic and social role for the organization. He encouraged India and Pakistan to remain part of the Commonwealth of Nations when they threatened to leave, and set a precedent by committing Canadian troops to overseas assignments during the crises in the Congo and Cyprus. St. Laurent was successful in negotiating Newfoundland's entry into Confederation on March 31, 1949.

The Prime Ministers of Canada

In 1951, St. Laurent brought in the old-age pension to every Canadian over the age of 70 and to those from ages 65 to 69 who needed it. He improved the relations between the English and French-speaking communities of Canada and enlarged Quebec's role in Canada's postwar boom. He abolished the practice of appeals to the Privy Council in Britain and made Canada's Supreme Court the final say on judicial matters in Canada. In 1952, he appointed the first Canadian-born Governor-General of Canada, Vincent Massey. In 1957, he established the Canada Council of the Arts which provided government subsidies for scholarship and creative arts. He also established the National Library of Canada in 1953 and set up the Department of Northern Affairs. He was instrumental in getting the United States to agree to build a system of locks and canals to complete the St. Lawrence Seaway in 1959.

As a result of his successful policies, his administration was returned to power twice with a majority government. He retired from politics in 1957 at the age of 75. He died in 1973 in Ottawa.

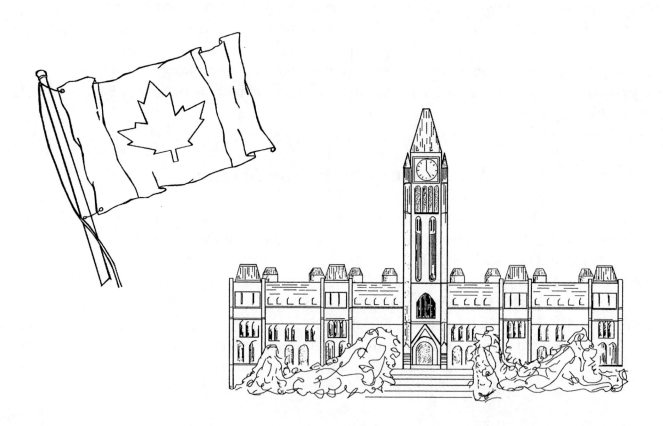

The Prime Ministers of Canada   *Louis Stephen St. Laurent*

Name _____ **Date** _____

Points to Ponder

1. Why was St. Laurent so old when he entered politics?
   _____
   _____

2. Why did King want him to become a member of Parliament?
   _____
   _____

3. What major accomplishment did he have as Attorney General?
   _____
   _____

4. Why did St. Laurent have an easier time as prime minister than those before him?
   _____
   _____

5. Name five of St. Laurent's accomplishments as prime minister.
   _____
   _____
   _____
   _____
   _____

 Explore History

1. Research the St. Lawrence Seaway. What places does it connect? Why was it important to both Canada and the United States?

2. What crises developed in the Congo and Cyprus?

3. Who was Vincent Massey? What qualifications did he have to be appointed as Governor-General?

The Prime Ministers of Canada

John George Diefenbaker (1895 - 1979)
Prime Minister: 1957 - 1963

John George Diefenbaker was born September 18, 1895, in Neustadt, Ontario, to a family of German-Scottish descent. The family left Ontario in 1903 to settle in Carlton, Saskatchewan, in 1906 to a homestead near Borden, and finally in 1910 they settled in Saskatoon so John and his brother could have a satisfactory education. In 1912, he entered the University of Saskatchewan where he gained renown as a great debater. He enrolled in the Canadian Officers Training Corps shortly after the outbreak of the First World War and was made a lieutenant in the Saskatoon Fusiliers after his graduation from university in 1916. He went overseas with the Canadian Expeditionary Force, but was injured and had to return home. He returned to university and completed a law degree in 1919. He had a small practice in the town of Wakaw, but soon gained a reputation throughout the province. In 1923, he moved to Prince Albert and set up a larger practice.

About the same time, Diefenbaker became interested in politics. He ran on five occasions in federal, provincial, and municipal elections, but lost each election. In 1940, he was elected as the member of Parliament for Lake Centre, Saskatchewan. His main concern was for the minorities and the individuals who had suffered injustice. He earned the reputation of being "the protector of the little man." Many of the causes he supported were unpopular, such as the confinement of the Japanese-Canadians during the Second World War.

He was passed over several times for the position of leader of the Conservative party, now known as the Conservative Party of Canada. His chance came in 1956 when George Drew resigned as leader. Diefenbaker was the strongest candidate and won the leadership on the first ballot. In the campaign for the election in 1957, Diefenbaker adopted many of the Liberal policies and added them to the vision of Canadian development. He gained new support in British Columbia, Ontario and the Maritimes. On June 21, 1957, he became prime minister.

The Prime Ministers of Canada

Diefenbaker as Prime Minister

In his first sitting of Parliament as prime minister, Diefenbaker saw to it that old-age pensions were increased, unemployment benefits were extended, taxes were cut, and new federal employment programs were introduced to help create new jobs. He appointed the first woman Cabinet minister, Elen Fairclough, in 1957, in 1958 the first Aboriginal Senator, James Gladstone then in 1959 the first French Canadian Governor-General, Georges Vanier. Diefenbaker called a surprise election in February, 1958 and his government won by the largest majority ever in Canadian history.

Diefenbaker's vision of Canada was that of development of the North. In 1958, a road-building and railway development was begun to bring the products of the North to southern markets. He also increased federal aid to universities and amateur sports. He was most proud of his Bill of Rights, which became law in 1960. This law barred discrimination in Canada on the basis of race or creed and was meant to apply to all federal legislation. However, since most aspects of civil rights were the responsibility of the provinces, the law had little effect.

Diefenbaker's popularity began to decline by 1960. In 1959, he had cancelled the development of a new fighter jet. That decision put fourteen thousand people out of work. In 1963, after a vote of non-confidence Diefenbaker resigned as prime minister. He stayed as a member of Parliament in the Opposition until his death in 1979.

The Prime Ministers of Canada *John George Diefenbaker*

Name _____ **Date** _____

Points to Ponder

1. How did Diefenbaker show that he was "the protector of the little man"?
   _____
   _____

2. How did Diefenbaker gain support in British Columbia and the Maritimes?
   _____
   _____

3. How did he plan to develop the North? Why?
   _____
   _____

4. What caused him to lose the popularity of the voters?
   _____
   _____

5. Why was the Bill of Rights not as effective as Diefenbaker had hoped?
   _____
   _____
   _____

 Explore History

1. It has been said that politics was the focus of Diefenbaker's life. Do you agree or disagree with this statement? Why?

2. Research the Canadian Bill of Rights. Prepare a poster explaining what this bill contains.

3. How were Japanese-Canadians treated during the Second World War? Why? What has happened recently because of this?

4. What is a vote of non-confidence in the government? How does it occur?

The Prime Ministers of Canada

Lester Bowles Pearson (1897 - 1972)
Prime Minister: 1963 - 1968

Lester Pearson was born April 23, 1897 in Newtonbrook (now part of North York), Ontario. He attended school in Peterborough and Hamilton, Ontario. He entered Victoria College in 1913, but left to enlist in the university's Ambulance Corps when the First World War broke out. Later, he joined the Canadian army and toward the end of the war, he became a commissioned flight lieutenant in the Royal Flying Corps. It was at this time he gained the nickname "Mike" which stuck with him throughout his life. He was injured on his first solo flight and returned home to become a training instructor. He resumed his studies after the war, and in 1923, he earned a history degree from Oxford and in 1924 was appointed lecturer at the University of Toronto. The following year he married one of his students, Maryon Moody. They had two children.

In 1928, he was persuaded by the head of the Department of External Affairs, Oscar Skelton, to take the foreign service examination. He excelled in the exam and was appointed to the position as first secretary of the department. This position allowed him to gain first-hand knowledge of international affairs as well as Canada's economic problems and national policies. In 1935, he went to London with Governor-General Vincent Massey, where he met many of the world's leading statesmen. He remained in London for the first part of the Second World War until he was recalled to Canada in 1941 to serve as assistant undersecretary of state for External Affairs. In 1945, he became ambassador to the United States.

Although he was active in political matters, Pearson did not enter politics until 1948. He was persuaded to stand for by-election in Quebec; he won the seat and was made minister for External Affairs. From 1943 to 1963, he served on many international committees and organizations including the United Nations. He initiated the resolution that ended the Suez crises and sent a UN police force to restore peace in the Gaza Strip. He designated certain battalions of the Canadian Armed Forces to serve as peacekeeping units. In 1957, he was awarded the Nobel Peace Prize, the first time this award had been given to a Canadian.

In the campaign for the election of 1963, Pearson proposed a Royal commission on biculturalism and bilingualism in Canada called the "Bi and Bi Commission." This suggestion greatly increased his popularity in Quebec. He also called for the addition of nuclear weapons to the Canadian arsenal. His party won the election, but had four seats short of a majority government. He called a new election, but only gained two extra seats.

The Prime Ministers of Canada

Pearson as Prime Minister

Pearson became Prime Minister on April 22, 1963. His government was in trouble from the start. His first budget put a high tax on foreign securities and raised tariffs which discouraged trade. He was later forced to cancel the changes. One major problem he had to face was the desire of French Canada for greater political autonomy and economic opportunity.

Extremist groups such as the Quebec Liberation Front were advocating that Quebec separate from Canada. He gave Quebec many generous subsidies and taxation arrangements and established the Royal Commission on Bilingualism and Biculturalism. In 1963, Pearson promised Canadians a new flag. His opponents saw this as a rejection of Britain. However, the Flag Bill was passed after bitter debate and on February 15, 1965, the new maple leaf flag flew over the Parliament Buildings in Ottawa.

In 1965, Pearson set up the Canada Pension Plan for retired workers, and in 1966, established Medicare, a health insurance plan for all Canadians. He also signed the Auto Pact with the United States in 1965, which allowed a fair share of Canadian-made cars to be sold in the United States. In 1967, he organized Expo '67, a birthday party held in Montreal for Canada's 100th birthday. The party lasted all year long. In 1967, he also created the Order of Canada to honour outstanding Canadians.

Pearson retired from politics in April, 1968. He died on December 27, 1972. In 1979, the United Nations created the Pearson Peace Medal to honour Canadians who follow Pearson's goal of trying to make the world a more peaceful place.

The Prime Ministers of Canada   *Lester Bowles Pearson*

Name _____ **Date** _____

Points to Ponder

1. How did Pearson gain his wide range of knowledge about politics?

2. What was the "Bi and Bi Commission"?

3. Why was he awarded the Nobel Peace Prize?

4. Give examples from Pearson's political career that show he was interested in helping Canadians.

5. How has the United Nations honoured Lester B. Pearson?

 Explore History

1. What is the Canada Pension plan? How does it benefit Canadians?

2. What is Medicare? When and why was it created?

3. What people have received the Pearson Medal of Honour since 1979?

4. What is the Nobel Peace Prize? What qualifications does one need to receive this prize? Give the names of three other people, besides Pearson, who have received this award.

The Prime Ministers of Canada

Pierre Elliott Trudeau (1919 - 2000)
Prime Minister: 1968 - 1979; 1980 - 1984

Joseph Phillippe Pierre Elliott Trudeau was born October 18, 1919, in Montreal, Quebec, the youngest of three children. He was educated at the Jesuit College Jean-de-Brebeuf, the University of Montreal, Harvard and the London School of Economics. He was admitted to the bar as a lawyer in 1943. From 1947 to 1949, he travelled extensively throughout the world, crossing five continents. Upon his return to Canada in 1949, he supported the unions in the bitter Asbestos Strike in Quebec. In 1956, he edited a book about the strike in which he included an introduction and a conclusion condemning the government of Maurice Duplessis in Quebec for its dominant social, economic and political policies. He developed a political philosophy centered on the need for individual liberty and social justice. He accused the Premier of corruption and resisting changes needed to modernize Quebec. He also criticized Prime Minister Pearson for his agreement to arm Canada with nuclear weapons, while campaigning for the New Democratic Party in the election of 1963.

In 1965, he was asked by Pearson to join the Liberal Party and run for Parliament representing the district of Mount Royal, Quebec. He won the election and went to Ottawa with two of his friends, Jean Marchand and Gerard Pelletier. Together in Parliament they were called Quebec's " Three Wise Men." He held the riding of Mount Royal until 1988. After two years in Parliament, Trudeau became a member of the Cabinet as Minister of Justice. He quickly gained a reputation as a reformer, bringing important changes to laws affecting divorce, homosexuality and abortion. He was chosen to be leader of the Party in 1968, and on April 20,1968, he became prime minister of Canada.

Trudeau as Prime Minister

In the election of 1968, Trudeau's Liberals swept the country by storm. "Trudeaumania" swept across Canada, as Canadians loved his dynamic, youthful image. He promised a "just" society for Canadians and a government which would be open to all Canadians. He wanted to appease the growing resentment between French and English-speaking Canadians, and was opposed to the growing separatist movement in Quebec. In 1969, his government passed the Official Languages Bill making both French and English the official languages of Canada. This meant that all government documents and signs would have to be printed in French as well as English. This act was unpopular in the western provinces where there were few French-speaking people.

The Prime Ministers of Canada

In October, 1970, a separatist group in Quebec calling itself the FLQ (Front de Liberation du Quebec) kidnapped, in Montreal, a British diplomat, James Cross, and a Quebec Cabinet Minister, Pierre Laporte. In spite of ransom demands, Trudeau refused to negotiate and invoked the War Measures Act to gain emergency powers for the government. On October 17, the murdered body of LaPorte was discovered and Cross was released by his captors in early December. The captors were tracked down and eventually served prison terms for their part in what has been called "The October Crisis." This event had long-term effects. It caused much resentment in Quebec and as a result the separatist movement intensified. Less controversial however, was Trudeau's creation in 1971 of the Canadian Development Corporation to purchase control of foreign companies with extensive holdings in Canada. In 1971, Trudeau met and married Margaret Sinclair.

Trudeau remained Prime Minister despite the 1972 election of a minority government. That year he appointed Muriel McQueen Fergusson as the first woman Speaker of the Senate. In 1973, he refused requests from the premiers of the four western provinces to seek a change in government policies. He also turned down Alberta's 1973 and 1974 requests to keep the profits of higher oil prices. The main problem of his second term of office was inflation. In 1974, the Conservatives voted against his government's budget because it failed to institute wage and price controls. Trudeau called an election for July and again was returned to power with a large majority.

During Trudeau's third term in office, Rene Levesque came to power as premier of Quebec. His aim was to have Quebec separate from Canada. Trudeau spoke out more than ever against an independent Quebec. This was also a time of economic trouble. In 1975, Trudeau imposed wage and price controls in spite of the fact that he had promised not to do so during his election campaign. He ended these controls in 1978, but many unemployed Canadians were disappointed with the Liberals. Trudeau remained as party leader after a brief interruption in November 1979 when he resigned as party leader, returned a month later again to take leadership of the Party. During his time in Opposition, he was often in Quebec urging people to choose to remain part of Canada.

In 1980, the Trudeau Liberals were again returned to power. He appointed Jeanne Sauve the first woman Speaker of the House of Commons. She became Canada's first female Governor-General in 1984. Trudeau called for a special vote or referendum to be held to allow the people of Quebec to vote on the separation issue. They voted to remain in Canada. Trudeau then turned his attention to giving Canadians their own constitution. He wanted to give Canadians basic rights and freedoms guaranteed by law. After much debate, the premiers of nine provinces agreed to the constitutional changes. The only exception was Quebec. The new Constitution became law on April 17, 1982. Trudeau spent the next two years trying to convince world leaders to reduce their stock of nuclear weapons. He resigned from office on February 29, 1984, but continued to speak out against actions of the government he did not agree with, particularly the Meech Lake and Charlottetown Accord agreements. He died on September 28, 2000. He had served as leader of a country longer than any other leader in the western world.

The Prime Ministers of Canada   *Pierre Elliott Trudeau*

Name _____ **Date** _____

Points to Ponder

1. What was "Trudeaumania"?
   _____
   _____

2. What "firsts" did Trudeau initiate for women in government?
   _____
   _____

3. Why did Trudeau want a Canadian constitution?
   _____
   _____

4. Why do you think Quebec would not agree to the changes in the Constitution?
   _____
   _____

5. Why did Trudeau call a referendum on the issue of Quebec separation?
   _____
   _____
   _____

 Explore History

1. What were the demands made by the FLQ in 1970? Who were the leaders of this organization?

2. What changes were made in the Canadian Constitution? Make a poster displaying the rights and freedoms of Canadian citizens.

3. Who was Rene Levesque? Research this person telling why he is so important in the history of Quebec.

4. Who is Jeanne Sauve? Why was she appointed as Governor-General?

The Prime Ministers of Canada

Charles Joseph Clark (b. 1939)
Prime Minister: June 4, 1979 - March 2, 1980

Charles Joseph (Joe) Clark was born June 5, 1939, in High River, Alberta, the son of a newspaper owner and editor. He began his political career as the National President of the Progressive Conservative (PC) Party at the University of Alberta. In this role, he developed a deep commitment to fostering political involvement among young people. He worked with Peter Lougheed to help build the Progressive Conservative Party in Alberta. The Party was elected to govern Alberta in 1971, and has governed the province ever since.

Joe Clark was elected to the House of Commons in 1972 as the member for Rocky Mountain, Alberta. He quickly distinguished himself as one of the hardest working and most effective members of Parliament. However, he remained virtually unknown in the rest of Canada until he was elected as the leader of the PC party in 1976. In May, 1979, his party defeated Trudeau's Liberals in the general election, and on June 4, 1979, Clark became the youngest Prime Minister of Canada at the age of 40.

Clark as Prime Minister

Clark had only a minority government but with the support of the New Democratic Party, he decided to proceed with selling off Petro-Canada and cut back government spending. This put the government-owned oil company on the road to privatization.

He appointed in 1979 the first Black Cabinet Minister, Lincoln Alexander, and was instrumental in seeing that American diplomats were sheltered at the Canadian embassy in Iran during the crisis of 1979 to 1980. His first budget in December of 1979, led by Minister of Finance John Crosbie, was defeated in the House of Commons. Clark called an election and was defeated by the Liberals. His term of office as prime minister lasted only nine months.

Clark remained in Opposition from 1980 to 1983, during which time he fought Trudeau's plans for a new constitution. He lost the leadership of the Party to Brian Mulroney at its 1983 convention. He then retired from politics but returned in 1998, replacing Jean Charest as leader of the PC Party. He won a seat in the House of Commons in September, 2000.

The Prime Ministers of Canada

John Napier Turner (b. 1929)
Prime Minister: June 30, 1984 - September 17, 1984

John Turner was born on June 7, 1929, in Richmond, Surrey, England. His father died when he was three and his mother took a job as an economist in the Canadian federal government. John grew up used to seeing politicians and dignitaries and chatted with prime ministers on occasion. He attended the University of British Columbia and won a Rhodes Scholarship to continue his studies in England. At university, he excelled in sports and was preparing to try out for the 1948 Olympics when a car accident ended his dream.

Turner returned to Canada in 1953 and became a lawyer in Montreal. He was brought into the Liberal Party by Lester Pearson and was elected to Parliament in 1962 at the age of 32. He joined the Cabinet in 1965. He ran for the leadership of the Liberal Party in 1968, but was defeated by Pierre Trudeau. From 1968 to 1972, he served as Minister of Justice in Trudeau's government sponsoring changes in the legal system. In 1975, he became Finance Minister, but after arguing with Trudeau over economic policy, he resigned from politics.

When Trudeau resigned in 1984, Turner ran for the leadership of the Liberal Party. This time he was successful. This also made him prime minister. He called an election and was defeated by Brian Mulroney. He served in the office of Prime Minister for 39 days – the second shortest period in Canadian history. He stayed on in Opposition fighting Mulroney's free trade plans, and retired from politics in 1990.

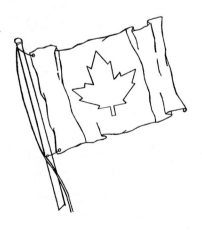

The Prime Ministers of Canada *Clark and Turner*

Name _____ **Date** _____

Points to Ponder

1. How did Joe Clark privatize government-owned oil companies?
   _____
   _____

2. What distinction does Clark hold among prime ministers of Canada?
   _____
   _____

3. What do Clark and Turner have in common regarding their terms in office?
   _____
   _____

4. Why did Turner resign from politics in 1975?
   _____
   _____

5. Why was John Turner at ease with government officials?
   _____
   _____

 Explore History

1. What were the newspaper headlines of the election of 1979? Why?

2. Why was Clark's budget defeated in 1980? Research this period of history and tell the major points which brought down his government.

3. What was the nepotism issue that helped the Conservatives defeat the Turner government in 1984?

4. What has John Turner done since retiring in 1990?

The Prime Ministers of Canada

Martin Brian Mulroney (b. 1939)
Prime Minister: 1984 - 1993

Martin Brian Mulroney was born March 20, 1939, in Baie-Comeau, Quebec, to a working class Irish family. He grew up speaking French and English. He attended boarding school in New Brunswick and studied at St. Francis Xavier University in Antigonish, Nova Scotia. It was here he first became involved in politics when he joined the Progressive Conservative Party. He returned to Quebec to study law and as a lawyer in Montreal, he specialized in labour relations. He was a commissioner on the Cliché Commission of Inquiry into the construction industry in Quebec where he uncovered corruption and violence in the industry. This was a high-profile report which made Mulroney well-known in Quebec. By 1961, he was an advisor to Prime Minister Diefenbaker and continued to work as an organizer for the PC Party.

In 1976, he ran for the leadership of the Party. He was defeated by Joe Clark, but later beat him in the leadership convention of 1983. He had no seat in Parliament and won the by-election for Central Nova, Nova Scotia. In the election of 1984, Mulroney became Prime Minister.

Mulroney as Prime Minister

Charges of scandal followed the Mulroney government for the first two years. He was portrayed as indecisive and his popularity declined. Midway through his term, he enacted three major policies. The first of these was free trade, which sparked heated debates in the House of Commons and resulted in the Canada - U.S. Free Trade agreement in 1988. The second policy was privatization. He began to sell off many crown corporations to private investors. He announced that Canada was "open for business". Mulroney's third policy was to make changes to Canada's Constitution, resulting in the Meech Lake Accord of 1987 which recognized Quebec as a distinct society.

He also introduced the Goods and Services Tax in 1991, a seven percent tax on products sold in Canada. The Meech Lake Accord was in jeopardy as three provinces withdrew their support from the plan, so he met with the premiers in Charlottetown in 1992. Together with Joe Clark, he worked out the Charlottetown Accord, but this was also rejected by Canadians.

He oversaw the deployment of Canadian troops to Kuwait and Saudi Arabia in the Gulf War in 1991, and negotiated a settlement with Nunavut which paved the way for this area to become a separate territory of Canada. However by 1993, Mulroney was the most unpopular prime minister ever in Canadian history. He resigned that spring and retired from political life.

The Prime Ministers of Canada

Avril Kim Campbell (b. 1947)
Prime Minister: June 25, 1993 - November 4, 1993

Avril Phaedra Douglas Campbell was born in Port Alberni, British Columbia on March 10, 1947. Shortly after she was born her parents moved to Vancouver so that her father could study law. Her mother left the family when Campbell was twelve years old. It was at this point she changed her name to Kim. She did well in school and became involved in politics at an early age, running and winning the presidency of the school student council. She became the first female president of Prince of Wales Secondary School.

In 1964, she attended the University of British Columbia where she majored in political science. She also was elected the first female freshman president. After graduation she won a scholarship to the London School of Economics where she began a doctorate degree in Soviet studies. She returned to Vancouver in 1973 to lecture part-time at Simon Fraser University and Vancouver Community College.

In 1980, she returned to university to study law and was elected to the Vancouver School Board. She ran as a Social Credit candidate in the provincial election of 1984, but lost the election. She was then offered a job as advisor to the premier of British Columbia, Bill Bennett. She was elected to the provincial legislature in 1986, but was approached by the Progressive Conservatives to run as a PC candidate in the federal election of 1988. She became Minister of State for Indian and Northern Affairs in 1989 and the following year she became Canada's first female Justice Minister. She introduced a bill amending gun laws, and had to balance the public outcry for more gun legislation with those who lobbied for the rights of gun owners following the Montreal Massacre.

She was praised for Bill C-49, a bill drafted to protect the rights of rape victims when the Supreme Court struck down the "rape shield" law as unconstitutional. In 1993, she became Minister of Defence and became embroiled in the EH-101 helicopter controversy and the deaths of four Somalis at the hands of the Canadian military. She was also successful in winning the leadership of the Conservative Party following the resignation of Brian Mulroney. She became Canada's first woman prime minister on June 25, 1993.

The Conservative mandate had run out and Campbell called an election for October 1993. The Progressive Conservative Party and Campbell herself were soundly defeated – returning only two Conservative members to the House of Commons. Campbell resigned as party leader and accepted a fellowship at Harvard University. She was recently appointed to the post of Consul General of Canada in Los Angeles, California.

The Prime Ministers of Canada   *Mulroney and Campbell*

Name _____ **Date** _____

Points to Ponder

1. How did Mulroney become well known in Quebec?
   _____
   _____

2. What were the three main issues of Mulroney's first term in office?
   _____
   _____
   _____

3. What were the Meech Lake and Charlottetown Accords?
   _____
   _____
   _____

4. What were Campbell's accomplishment as a member of Parliament?
   _____
   _____
   _____

5. Why is it that she did not have any achievements as prime minister of Canada?
   _____
   _____

 Explore History

1. What were the terms of the Meech Lake Accord?
2. What was the Cliché Commission? What was the result?
3. What was Bill C-49? How did it affect Canadian Law?
4. What was the EH-101 helicopter controversy?
5. What part did Canadians play in the peacekeeping efforts in Somalia?

The Prime Ministers of Canada

Jean Chrétien (b. 1934)
Prime Minister: 1993 - 2003

Joesph Jacques Jean Chrétien was born on January 11, 1934, in Shawinigan, Quebec, the eighteenth child of a paper mill machinist. Although his academic achievements were modest, his parents were determined to give him a good education. He attended boarding school in Trois-Rivières and even though he was a good student, he was homesick and found the discipline of the school too strict. He also had to cope with deafness in one ear and a paralysis of the left side of his face caused by a childhood illness. He developed an interest in politics at a young age as his father was an organizer for the Liberal Party. Jean helped him distribute pamphlets and attended political rallies. While studying law at Laval, he joined the campus Liberal Club.

He campaigned for several Liberal leaders in Quebec, and in 1963 he was asked to run as the Liberal candidate for St. Maurice-Laflèche in the federal election. In a hard fought campaign, Chrétien won the seat. He spent his first two years in Parliament as a backbencher improving his English. In 1965, he was appointed parliamentary secretary under Minister of Finance Mitchell Sharp. In 1968, Prime Minister Trudeau made him Minister of National Revenue and later Minister of Indian and Northern Affairs. He created a policy paper on Native issues in 1969. In 1972, he set up the Berger Commission to make recommendations on a proposed pipeline in the Mackenzie River Valley, and established an office for the settling of Native land claims. He also created ten new national parks during his six years as minister.

In 1974, he served as President of the Treasury Board and then moved to Industry, Trade and Commerce in 1976, where he financed the development of the Challenger aircraft. In 1977, he became Minister of Finance, overseeing the removal of wage and price controls that had been put into effect in 1975. In 1980, he became Minister of Justice where he was responsible for supporting the "No" forces in the Quebec referendum. He also drafted and organized the passage of the 1982 Charter of Rights and the new Canadian Constitution. That year he appointed Bertha Wilson as the first woman Justice of the Supreme Court of Canada.

He ran for leadership of the Liberal Party after Trudeau's resignation in 1984. He was defeated because he had been associated with Trudeau. Chrétien served as deputy prime minister for two months and then resigned in 1986 to return to practicing law. When John Turner left politics in 1990, Chrétien again ran for the leadership of the Party. This time he was successful and in the election of 1993, he led the Liberals to a majority government. He became Prime Minister of Canada on November 4, 1993.

The Prime Ministers of Canada

Chrétien as Prime Minister

Chrétien, in his term as prime minister, held another referendum on the issue of Quebec separation when a very slim majority voted against Quebec independence. He promised to abolish the GST, but this tax is still in existence at printing. He led "Team Canada", made up of business leaders, on trips to other countries to encourage and create world trade with Canada. He passed new gun control laws in 1996.

His government was committed to reducing the deficit – the money Canada owed because it has had to borrow money to pay for the many services for its people. He reduced the amount of income tax which Canadian taxpayers had to pay, but at the same time he supervised cuts to social programs in Canada in order to try to pay down this debt. Health, education, and unemployment insurance experienced cutbacks.

Chrétien was a world leader in military matters as well. He often conferred with Canada's allies on threats of terrorism, the Middle East Crisis between Israel and Palestine and the situation in Iraq under Saddam Hussein. He attended all world meetings in an attempt to bring Canada's opinions to the world stage. He was a strong supporter of NAFTA – the North American Free Trade Agreement – which allowed freer trade between Canada, the U.S., and Mexico. Chrétien regarded this agreement as being much more than reduced tariffs. He said it was about dispute settlement, national treatment, procurement codes, transparency and impartiality. He said it created a rules-based system for traders and inventors. He believed that such an agreement could build new prosperity for Canada, create more jobs and enhance the quality of life for Canadians.

Jean Chrétien was a strong supporter of the Kyoto Accord. This accord called for 40 industrialized countries to make sharp reductions in greenhouse gas emissions, which is causing global warming, by 2012. Many Canadians did not support Chrétien's position on this matter, especially business people, who argued that such an agreement would cost Canadians thousands of jobs and billions of dollars. The fact that the Accord was not supported by the United States, the biggest buyer of Canada's energy products, was the basis for the disagreement with Canada's support of the Accord.

Jean Chrétien had encountered much dissent within the Liberal Party. Many Liberals called for a leadership review, in the hope that Chrétien would be ousted as the leader of the Party. Chrétien, in late August, 2002, announced that as of February, 2004, he would retire from political life.

The Prime Ministers of Canada *Jean Chrétien*

Name _____ Date _____

Points to Ponder

1. What did Jean Chrétien accomplish as a minister in the cabinet?

2. What was the Berger Commission?

3. How did Chrétien's experience as a member of the cabinet prepare him for his role as prime minister?

4. What is "Team Canada"?

5. What was the result of the second Quebec Referendum?

6. What is the Kyoto Accord? What are the arguments for and against this agreement?

 Explore History

1. Why do separatists in Quebec want to leave Canada? What are the arguments they use?

2. What are the names of the ten new national parks created by Chrétien?

3. Chrétien spent two years as a backbencher. What does this mean?

4. Jean Chrétien has had many disagreements with several of his top Cabinet ministers, namely Brian Tobin and Paul Martin. What were these disagreements about?

5. Who is your representative in the current House of Commons? When was he/she elected?

The Prime Ministers of Canada

Paul Edgar Philippe Martin (b. 1938)
Prime Minister: 2003 – 2006

Paul Martin was born on August 28, 1938, in Windsor, Ontario, the first of two children of Nell and Paul Martin Sr., a Liberal politician. For the first few years of his life, Paul, his sister and parents lived in Windsor, Ontario until his father became a minister in the government and the family moved to Ottawa. In the summer of 1946, Paul was rushed to hospital with polio, paralyzed in the throat and unable to speak. This crisis passed, although it did take a year for him to fully recover. Despite the fact that the illness in the end was not as serious as it might have been, in later life, Paul Martin is known to have said that the odds were not in his favour. Most people stricken with polio at that time, died or ended up in an iron lung, and he was very fortunate to have had a full recovery. In 1957, Paul Jr. enrolled at St. Michael's College at the University of Toronto, following in the footsteps of his father, to study philosophy. After graduating with a Bachelor of Arts in 1961, Paul enrolled in Osgoode Hall Law School where he received his Bachelor of Laws (LLB) degree in 1964. He was called to the Ontario bar in 1966.

Paul was introduced to politics early in life and did, on occasion, travel around the riding on weekends with his father. While at university he was asked to join the university Liberal Club. He often insisted that politics did not fit into his life plans. In 1966, he joined Canada Steamship Lines as an assistant, and worked his way up to an executive level position. In 1981, Martin purchased Power Corp.

He became more politically involved in 1988 when he was asked to run as the Liberal candidate for the Montreal riding of LaSalle-Emard. In 1990, he ran for the leadership of the Canadian Liberal Party, but was defeated by Jean Chrétien. For the years 1991 to 1993, he was the finance critic and critic for the environment in Liberal opposition. When the Liberals won the election in 1993, Paul Martin became the Minister responsible for Quebec Regional Development, 1993 to 1996. He became Minister of Finance in 1993 until 2002 when he left the Liberal Party to run for the leadership of the party.

In November 2003, Paul Martin, with an unprecedented majority, won the Liberal leadership, and was sworn in as Canada's 22nd Prime Minister on December 12, 2003.

The Prime Ministers of Canada

Martin as Prime Minister

After only a few months as Prime Minister, Paul Martin's government erupted with scandal. A report from the Auditor General suggested that millions of dollars were given to businesses in Quebec that were friendly to the Liberals in exchange for work contracts for various projects in Quebec. But much of the work that was commissioned was never done. Martin called an official inquiry into the Sponsorship Scandal, however, the scandal reduced Paul Martin's popularity, particularly in Quebec. Martin had to call an election, and did so in June 2004, winning narrowly and ushering in an unstable minority government.

From the start, the Conservatives, Bloc Québécois, and New Democratic Party cooperated to control the actions of the Liberal government; first by forcing amendments to the Speech from the Throne. Nonetheless Martin's government had some impact on Canada, seeing increases to healthcare, addressing some of the imbalances between provinces in their financial wellbeing, and pushing through the Civil Marriage Act, which legalized same-sex marriage. Canada is the fourth country in the world to do so. Martin declined Canada's participation in the Amercian National Missile Defence Program and was criticized for not providing more money to other foreign countries in need of aid.

In February 2005, Martin revealed his government's plans for improvements to Canada's childcare, military, and the environment in the new budget. The budget nearly didn't get through the House of Commons though, as the other parties saught to join forces to shut down Martin's government with "a vote of no confidence". The vote to pass the budget was in fact tied, and the Speaker of the House of Commons was called upon to break it, voting in the favour of maintaining government, as is the tradition.

In November, the first results from the Gomery Inquiry into the Sponsorship Scandal were released. The Inquiry decided that Paul Martin was not responsible for any wrongdoing. Shortly thereafter, the Conservatives, Bloc Québécois, and New Democratic Party cooperated in a motion of non confidence which dissolved the government, forcing an election on January 23rd, 2006.

The Liberal Party was defeated by the Conservative Party of Canada, and Paul Martin stepped down as leader of the Liberals. After a rocky term as prime minister, he remains a member of Parliament for his riding, LaSalle-Émard, Quebec.

The Prime Ministers of Canada *Paul Martin*

Name _____ Date _____

Points to Ponder

1. What experiences prepared Paul Martin for a life in politics?
   _____
   _____
   _____

2. As Minister of Finance, what was Paul Martin's biggest accomplishment?
   _____
   _____

3. What were the key priorities of the Paul Martin government?
   _____
   _____
   _____

4. Of the things Paul Martin tried to change about Canada, what do you think is a good idea? What, in your view, is a bad idea?
   _____
   _____
   _____
   _____

 Explore History

1. What is a vote of no confidence? Where and when did this tradition originate?

2. Paul Martin was Chairman of the G-20. What is the G-20? Which countries are involved?

3. The Sponsorship Scandal had a very negative impact on Paul Martin's government. What did the people involved do wrong?

The Prime Ministers of Canada

Stephen Joseph Harper (b. 1959)
Prime Minister: 2006 –

Stephen Harper was born on April 30th, 1959 to parents Margaret Johnstone and Joseph Harper in Toronto, Ontario, where he grew up with two younger brothers. He went to high school at Richmond Collegiate Institute in Etobicoke, and graduated top student in his year. Stephen started university at the University of Toronto, but left to move out to Edmonton where he took a job as a computer programmer. He then went to the University of Calgary, and completed a Master's degree in Economics.

Stephen was a member of the Liberal Club in high school, but changed his allegiance because he disagreed with some of Trudeau's policies. He became an aide to the Progressive Conservative Jim Hawkes in 1985, but was dissappointed by the Mulroney government and left the Party in 1986. With encouragement from Preston Manning, Stephen joined the Reform Party, becoming their Chief Policy Officer in 1987. He ran for the Calgary West seat in 1987, squarely losing to his former employer, Jim Hawkes. He tried again for the same seat in the 1993 election, and won. That same year he married Laureen Teskey; they now have two children.

Stephen resigned as a member of parliament in 1997, due to differences with the Reform Party leader, Preston Manning. He became president of the National Citizens Coalition, a conservative organization, and co-wrote *Our Benign Dictatorship* which suggests that Canada's government has been prominently Liberal for so long because the conservative parties in Canada were divided. In 2002, Stephen was elected leader of the Canadian Alliance Party, which evolved from the former Reform Party. He ran in a by-election in Calgary Southwest to become a member of Parliament and Leader of the Opposition. He worked for 18 months to unite the conservatives of the Alliance and Progressive Conservative parties into a new party – the Conservative Party of Canada. In 2004, he ran for leadership of this new party and won easily.

Stephen Harper believes in low taxes, federalism, and giving provinces more power, but not making special concessions to Quebec. In his election campaign, he promised to lower taxes, and to create laws that limit the chances of governments being dishonest, such as in the Sponsorship Scandal. He wants to change the Liberal federal childcare program, and provide some money to families with children to use for child care however they wish. Some people say that the money is not enough to help people to look after their young children. He also wants to change the criminal laws so there are guaranteed minimum sentences for serious crimes, to improve relations with the United States, and to work with provinces to ensure that patients needing health care like surgeries do not have to wait too long.

Stephen Harper is considered to be a smart man that holds strong beliefs. He also shares many of the same challenges and pleasures that other Canadians do. He has asthma, and loves hockey – especially the Calgary Flames. He is even writing a book on the history of the sport.

The Prime Ministers of Canada　　　　　　　　　　　　　　　　　　*Stephen Harper*

Name _____ **Date** _____

Points to Ponder

1. What was Stephen Harper's first job in politics?
   _____
   _____

2. Stephen Harper resigned from a position several times. Why do you think that is?
   _____
   _____

3. What does *The Benign Dictatorship* say about why Liberals were in power in Canada for so long?
   _____
   _____

4. What about Stephen Harper's child care policy do some people like? What do the critics of the child care policy say?
   _____
   _____
   _____
   _____

 Explore History

1. Stephen Harper has been called idealogical by his colleagues. What does this mean?

2. Has Stephen Harper restructured the government? What has he changed?

3. One of the things that Stephen Harper aims to do is improve relations with the United States. Why is this an issue for Canada?

The Prime Ministers of Canada

What Have You Learned?

Name _____   Date _____

Complete the following table of the prime ministers of Canada.

	Party	Dates	Occupation
John A. Macdonald			
A. Mackenzie			
John Abbott			
John Thompson			
Mackenzie Bowell			
Charles Tupper			
Wilfrid Laurier			
Robert Borden			
Arthur Meighen			
W.L.M. King			
Richard Bennett			
Louis St. Laurent			
John Diefenbaker			
Lester Pearson			
Pierre Trudeau			
Joe Clark			
John Turner			
Brian Mulroney			
Kim Campbell			
Jean Chrétien			
Paul Martin			
Stephen Harper			

The Prime Ministers of Canada
Quiz 1

Name _____ Date _____

Circle the letter with the correct answer beside it:

1. Before becoming a politician, John A. Macdonald was a
   a) farmer
   b) writer
   c) lawyer
   d) doctor

2. Sir John A. Macdonald resigned because of the
   a) Pacific Scandal
   b) Red River Rebellion
   c) Quebec Referendum
   d) the St. Lawrence Seaway

3. Alexander Mackenzie was originally from
   a) England
   b) Scotland
   c) Germany
   c) United States

4. Sir John Abbott was _____ years old when he became prime minister.
   a) 39
   b) 63
   c) 57
   d) 70

5. In 1892, Thompson passed the
   a) Medicare Act
   b) Canada Pensions Act
   c) Criminal Code
   d) Unemployment Insurance

6. Mackenzie Bowell's first job was as a
   a) newspaper editor
   b) farmer
   c) writer
   c) fisherman

7. Sir Charles Tupper was from
   a) Newfoundland
   b) Nova Scotia
   c) Quebec
   d) New Brunswick

8. The British North America Act was drafted by
   a) Mackenzie King
   b) Pierre Trudeau
   b) Brian Mulroney
   d) John A. Macdonald

9. Which of the following was created under Sir Wilfrid Laurier?
   a) British Columbia
   b) Yukon Territory
   c) Manitoba
   c) Nova Scotia

© S&S Learning Materials

The Prime Ministers of Canada Quiz 1

10. Borden passed the _____ while in office.
   a) Naval Service Bill
   b) Constitution Amendment
   c) War Measures Act
   d) British North America Act

11. Meighen became prime minister for a second term after the
   a) Pacific Scandal
   b) War Measures Act
   c) Bi and Bi Commission
   d) Customs Scandal

12. Mackenzie King brought _____ to Canada.
   a) Medicare
   b) Unemployment Insurance
   c) Canada Pension
   d) Bilingualism

13. Louis St. Laurent negotiated _____'s entry into Confederation.
   a) Alberta
   bo) Newfoundland
   c) Saskatchewan
   d) Prince Edward Island

14. Diefenbaker introduced the
   a) Medicare Act
   b) Bill of Rights
   c) War Measures Act
   d) Criminal Code of Canada

15. Leaster Pearson was the first Canadian to receive
   a) knighthood from the Queen
   b) the Pearson Peace Medal
   c) the Nobel Peace Prize
   d) a membership in the Privy Council

16. Trudeau was once known as one of the
   a) Rat Pack
   b) Three Wise Men
   c) radicals in Parliament
   d) Quebec Separatists

17. Brian Mulroney worked out the
   a) Meech Lake Accord
   b) Canadian Constitution
   c) War Measures Act
   d) Canada Pension Plan

18. Kim Campbell helped to pass
   a) Bill 101
   b) Bill 609
   c) Bill C - 49
   d) Bill C - 34

19. Jean Chrétien became prime minister in
   a) 1996
   b) 1984
   c) 1992
   d) 1993

20. _____ was the prime minister who legalized same-sex marriage.
   a) Brian Mulroney
   b) Jean Chrétien
   c) Paul Martin
   d) Stephen Harper

The Prime Ministers of Canada

Quiz 2

Name _____ Date _____

A. Which Prime Minister served during these crises?

1. ____ the First World War   a) Brian Mulroney
2. ____ the Boer War   b) Pierre Trudeau
3. ____ the Gulf War   c) Wilfrid Laurier
4. ____ the Second World War   d) Robert Borden
5. ____ the October Crisis   e) Mackenzie King

B. Which prime minister matches each of these milestones?

1. _____ appointed the first Canadian Governor-General.

2. _____ was the first French Canadian prime minister.

3. _____ had the shortest term as prime minister.

4. _____ appointed the first Auditor General.

5. _____ was the first woman prime minister.

6. _____ was the first prime minister appointed from the Senate.

7. _____ approved the maple leaf as the National flag of Canada.

8. _____ appointed the first woman Governor-General.

9. _____ created the first Canadian national park.

10. _____ appointed the first woman to the Senate.

a) Sir John A. Macdonald   b) Sir John Abbott   c) W. L. M. King
d) Alexander Mackenzie   e) Wilfrid Laurier   f) Louis St. Laurent
g) Kim Campbell   h) Pierre Trudeau   i) Charles Tupper
j) Lester Pearson

The Prime Ministers of Canada

Answer Key

Becoming a Prime Minister: *(page 9)*
1. It means "first among equals".
2. The prime minister of Canada is the leader of the party which obtains the most seats in the House of Commons in a general election. He/She is then appointed prime minister by the Governor-General.
3. The prime minister is: **a.** government leader   **b.** Cabinet leader   **c.** a member of Parliament   **d.** Party leader   **e.** international leader
4. Answers may vary.

Sir John A. Macdonald: *(page 12)*
1. He earned a reputation for flair and ingenuity in his work.
2. He was opposed to Responsible Government and Confederation.
3. He was willing to work with the French Canadians in order to broaden the Conservative Party and encourage more people to join it.
4. The accomplishments of Macdonald were: 1. He arranged better terms of union for Nova Scotia. 2. He bought land from the Hudson's Bay Company.
3. He added Manitoba, the Northwest Territories, British Columbia and Prince Edward Island to Canada.
4. He created the Northwest Mounted Police.   5. He oversaw the completion of the Canadian Pacific Railway.
6. He established the National Policy.

Alexander Mackenzie: *(page 15)*
1. He came to Canada because of a shortage of work in Scotland and because his fiancee had emigrated there with her family.
2. He built the Welland Canal, the Martello Towers at Fort Henry, a church and bank in Sarnia, and the courthouses and jails in Chatham and Sandwich.
3. As prime minister, he oversaw the completion of the Intercolonial Railway, the completion of the Parliament buildings, the introduction of the secret ballot, founded the Royal Military College, created the office of the Auditor General and offered amnesty to Louis Riel.
4. He was a sensible, honest and hardworking individual.
5. His honesty would not let him allow contractors to take their usual profits or give contracts to Liberals.

Sir John Joseph Caldwell Abbott: *(page 18)*
1. He was the first prime minister to be appointed from the Senate and the first one to be born in Canada.
2. He redistributed the parliamentary seats, reorganized the offices of Customs and Inland Revenue, created the Department of Trade and Commerce, revised the Criminal Code, and signed a Reciprocity Treaty with the United States.
3. It was from his office that the documents that started the Pacific Scandal were stolen.
4. He switched allegiance from the Conservatives to the Liberals because he supported Confederation.
5. The Annexation Manifesto was a bill that Abbott signed advising the British North American colonies give up their connection to Britain. As a result, Britain removed all preferential tariffs on colonial products and Abbott became very unpopular with voters.

Sir John Sparrow David Thompson: *(page 21)*
1. His duties gave him a first hand knowledge of how Parliament worked.
2. He was convinced by the bishop to run for election in a by-election in 1877.
3. He was approached by Sir John A. Macdonald to run in the federal riding of Antigonish.
4. He was involved in sentencing Louis Riel for treason and in negotiating a treaty with the United States.
5. Answers may vary.

MacKenzie Bowell: *(page 23)*
1. Answers may vary.
2. His hometown of Belleville was a growing manufacturing town.
3. He said that if Britain expected Canada to give its goods preferential treatment, then Canada should expect the same from Britain over U.S. goods or goods from other countries.
4. He was seventy years old and too old to do a good job.

Sir Charles Tupper: *(page 25)*
1. Through his medical practice, he had made a lot of politically influential friends.
2. He reorganized the province's education system.
3. The original intention was to form a confederation of the Atlantic colonies.
4. He stepped aside to allow a fair representation of Protestants and Catholics.
5. He chose to stay in London as the Canadian High Commissioner.
6. The term of office for the Conservatives was up and he had to call an election.

Sir Wilfrid Laurier: *(page 29)*
1. They were opposed to him because he was a member of a group that was not endorsed by the Roman Catholic church. He defended his right to hold political beliefs not endorsed by the clergy.
2. In his first speech in Parliament, he stressed that his liberalism was not of the type opposed to the Pope.
3. He set up a system in the schools that allowed a limited amount of religious teaching and instruction in the French language.
4. He offered Britain imperial preference on all its trade with Canada.
5. He believed that the British representative should have sided with Canada instead of the United States, and that Canada should have the power to solve its own problems.
6. He created the territory of Yukon and the provinces of Saskatchewan and Alberta, created the departments of Labour and External Affairs, introduced the Naval Service Bill and worked out a Reciprocity Treaty with the United States.

Sir Robert Laird Borden: *(page 32)*
1. He did not like the lack of rational debate, the hypocrisy and the politicking that existed in Parliament. He spoke out against the things he disagreed with, often speaking out against his own party.
2. He moved to Ottawa and gave up his law practice.
3. The Halifax Manifesto was a document in which Borden set out what he believed to be the proper aims of the Conservative party. These included a reform of the Senate, stricter supervision of immigration, nationalization of the communication systems, regulation of the public utilities, a protective tariff, and government control of the resources of the West.
4. Answers may vary.
5. It gave Parliament the power to censure the media, arrest people on suspicion, imprison people without trial, and take control of communications and transportation.
6. He gained international recognition for Canada by helping to establish the League of Nations and insisting that peace treaties be signed by Canada separate from Britain.

Arthur Meighen: *(page 35)*
1. The first controversy Meighen was involved in was Prime Minister Borden's attempt to push his own Naval Bill through the House of Commons and the Senate.
2. These bills were unpopular because they took away the right to vote from people who were seen as objecting to the government's conscription bill and those who were seen as enemies of the country.
3. He ordered a violent put down of the strikers.
4. He organized the government take-over of the railways.
5. He refused to renew a treaty with Britain unless all countries bordering the Pacific were included.

William Lyon Mackenzie King: *(page 39)*
1. He did a report on the Canadian garment industry and found that the companies making the uniforms for the Canadian Post Office were the worst offenders in terms of labour practices. He gave the information to the Postmaster General and it was because of this he was invited to be Deputy Mminister of Labour.
2. He wrote about his beliefs on capitalism and labour. He advocated more cooperation between community, labour and companies, and recommended a larger share of the control of capital by the government.
3. To avoid controversial issues, King tended to refer such things to be voted on by Parliament. An example of this is when Britain wanted Canada to support it in its threatened war against Turkey.
4. He introduced conscription for an army that would stay home to defend the country if needed.
5. When Britain tried to set up a foreign defense policy, King refused to cooperate and by doing this he ensured that Canada was recognized as an independent country.

Richard Bradford Bennett: *(page 42)*
1. Answers may vary.
2. He was the first party leader to be elected in a Leadership Convention and he was the first prime minister to make full use of the civil service.
3. He introduced the Statute of Westminster, giving Canada power to amend its own constitution, negotiated the St. Lawrence Deep Waterways Treaty with the United States, created the CBC and established the Bank of Canada.
4. Answers may vary.
5. He used personnel from various departments to draft legislation, negotiate trade agreements or to act as economic advisors.

Louis St. Laurent: *(page 45)*
1. He was 59 years of age.
2. He needed a person to handle Quebec politics.
3. He played a major role in uncovering an elaborate spy ring operating in Canada which allegedly passed Canadian nuclear secrets to the Soviets.
4. The Canadian economy was healthy in the years following the Second World War making it easier to be prime minister during this period.
5. As prime minister, St. Laurent negotiated Newfoundland's entry into Confederation, brought in old-age pensions, made the Supreme Court the final say on judicial matters, appointed the first Canadian-born Governor-General, established the Council of the Arts and the National Library of Canada and set up the Department of Northern Affairs.

John George Diefenbaker: *(page 48)*
1. As prime minister, most of his acts had to do with improving the life of ordinary Canadians such as creating federal programs to help people find jobs, increasing the amounts of money for old age pensions and unemployment insurance and cutting taxes.
2. He adopted many of the policies of the Liberals and added them to his vision of the development of Canada.
3. He planned to develop the North by building new railways and roads to bring the products of the North to markets in the South.
4. In 1959, he cancelled the order for a new fighter jet. This action put fourteen thousand people out of work.
5. It was not as effective as he had hoped because most of the aspects of civil rights were the responsibility of the provinces.

Lester Pearson: *(page 51)*
1. He was appointed to the position of first secretary of the Department of External Affairs.
2. The Bi and Bi Commission was a Royal Commission set up to look into relations between French- and English-speaking Canadians. It refers to bilingualism and biculturalism.
3. He was awarded the Nobel Peace Prize in recognition for all that he had done to bring peace to various areas of the world.
4. He established the Canada Pension Plan, Medicare and signed the Auto Pact with the United States.
5. It created the Pearson Peace Medal to be awarded to Canadians who follow in his footsteps of trying to bring peace to the world.

Pierre Elliott Trudeau: *(page 54)*
1. "Trudeaumania" is the term given to the craze that swept Canada because voters were enthusiastic about having a young and dynamic leader.
2. He appointed the first woman to the Senate and appointed the first woman Governor-General.
3. He wanted to give Canadians basic rights and freedoms guaranteed by the laws of their own country.
4. Answers may vary.
5. He wanted to see if the majority of Quebecers really wanted to separate, and if they didn't, to show the Quebec leaders they didn't have the support of the majority of the people.

Clark and Turner: *(page 57)*
1. He sold the government-owned oil companies to private companies.
2. He was the youngest prime minister of Canada.
3. They both served very short terms.

4. He resigned because he did not agree with Trudeau's economic policy.
5. He grew up surrounded by government officials and was used to talking with them.

Mulroney and Campbell: *(page 60)*
1. He was a commissioner on the Cliché Commission which uncovered scandal and corruption in the Quebec construction industry.
2. The three main issues were free trade, the selling of many Crown corporations and amendments to the Constitution.
3. They were intended to be amendments to the Constitution which would help breach the distance between Quebec and the other provinces and to enable Quebec to sign the Canadian Constitution.
4. She introduced gun legislation and drafted Bill C-49 which dealt with rape victims.
5. The term of office for the Conservatives was up when she became prime minister, so she had to call an election.

Jean Chrétien: *(page 63)*
1. He set up ten new national parks, established the Berger Commission, established an office for settling Native land claims, financed the development of the Challenger aircraft, drafted the 1982 Charter of Rights and Freedoms and appointed the first woman to the Supreme Court of Canada.
2. The Berger Commission was set up to study the possibility of having a pipeline in the Mackenzie River Valley.
3. He had been a part of so many departments that he had a vast knowledge of the workings of each one when he became prime minister.
4. "Team Canada" is a group of industrial leaders and company owners who travel with the Prime Minister to various countries of the world, trying to establish new markets for Canadian products.
5. The result of the second Quebec referendum was that a slim majority of Quebecers voted to stay in Canada.
6. The Kyoto Accord is an attempt on the part of 40 industrialized countries of the world to make an agreement to cut energy emissions into the atmosphere by the year 2012. The arguments for this agreement are that it is necessary to prevent large destruction of life due to intense global warming, help the environment, and preserve the atmosphere by cutting down pollution. The arguments against are that it will cause the loss of thousands of jobs and the countries will lose millions of dollars.

Paul Martin: *(page 66)*
1. His father was a politician. Paul grew up surrounded by politics, accompanied his father on weekend trips through the riding, and took a leave of absence from his job so that he could help run his father's leadership campaign.
2. As Finance Minister, Paul Martin reduced the deficit by making drastic cuts to federal government spending, which resulted in deficit-free budgets for the Government of Canada between 1997 and 2002.
3. Social Policy: health care, early childhood development, homelessness, and the quality of life for seniors. Economic Policy: sound government fiscal management; ongoing reviews for federal government programs. Foreign Policy and Security: developing national security.
4. Answers may vary.

Stephen Harper: *(page 68)*
1. He was an aide to the Progressive Conservative Jim Hawkes from 1985-1986.
2. Answers may vary. (e.g. When he believes in something strongly, he doesn't compromise on those beliefs.)
3. It says that Liberals have been in power because the conservative people in the country have been split into different political parties by differences in opinion.
4. Those who like Stephen's child care policy think it is a good idea to give parents the choice about how they take care of their children, and being given money from the government helps them to do that. Those who do not like the idea think that the government should instead build a good daycare system, so that there is somewhere for Canadian children to get good quality day care; they say that the money Stephen Harper plans to give parents won't be enough.

What Have You Learned: *(page 69)*

Party	Dates	Occupation
John A. Macdonald - Liberal - Conservative	1867 - 1873/1878 -1891	Lawyer
A. Mackenzie - Liberal	1873 - 1878	Contractor, Editor
John Abbott Liberal - Conservative	1891 -1892	Lawyer
John Thompson-Liberal - Conservative	1892 - 1894	Lawyer
Mackenzie Bowell - Conservative	1894 - 1896	Editor, Printer
Charles Tupper - Conservative	1896	Doctor
Wilfrid Laurier - Liberal	1896 - 1911	Lawyer
Robert Borden - Conservative	1911 -1920	Lawyer
Arthur Meighen - Liberal	1920 - 1921/1926	Lawyer
W. L. M. King - Liberal	1921 - 1930/1935 - 1948	Lawyer
Richard Bennett - Conservative	1930 - 1935	Lawyer
Louis St. Laurent - Liberal	1948 - 1957	Lawyer
John Diefenbaker - Progressive Conservative	1957 - 1963	Lawyer
Lester Pearson - Liberal	1963 - 1968	Professor
Pierre Trudeau - Liberal	1968 - 1979/1980 - 1984	Lawyer
Charles (Joe) Clark - Progressive Conservative	1979 - 1980	Journalist
John Turner - Liberal	1984	Lawyer
Brian Mulroney - Progressive Conservative	1984 - 1993	Lawyer
A. Kim Campbell - Progressive Conservative	1993	Lawyer
Jean Chrétien - Liberal	1993	Lawyer
Paul Martin - Liberal	2003 - 2006	Lawyer
Stephen Harper - Conservative	2006 -	Economist

Quiz 1: *(page 70)*
1. c   2. a   3. b   4. d   5. c   6. a   7. b   8. d   9. b   10. a   11. d   12. b   13. b   14. b   15. c
16. b   17. a   18. c   19. d   20. c

Quiz 2: *(page 72)*
Part A
1. d   2. c   3. a   4. e   5. b

Part B
1. f   2. e   3. i   4. d   5. g   6. b   7. j   8. h   9. a   10. c

Sir John A. Macdonald
1815-1891

Alexander Mackenzie
1822-1892

Sir John Joseph Caldwell Abbott
1821-1893

Sir John Sparrow David Thompson
1845-1894

Mackenzie Bowell
1823-1917

Sir Charles Tupper
1821-1915

Sir Wilfrid Laurier
1841-1919

Sir Robert Laird Borden
1854-1937

Arthur Meighen
1874-1960

William Lyon Mackenzie King
1874-1950

Richard Bedford Bennett
1870-1947

Louis Stephen St. Laruent
1882-1973

John George Diefenbaker
1895-1979

Lester Bowles Pearson
1897-1972

Pierre Elliott Trudeau
1919-2000

Charles Joseph Clark
b. 1939

John Napier Turner
b. 1929

Martin Brian Mulroney
b. 1939

Avril Kim Campbell
b. 1947

Jean Chrétien
b. 1934

Paul Martin
b. 1938

Stephen Joseph Harper
b. 1959

Who will be the next Prime Minister?